SIDE HUSTLE LAW

9 Essential Lessons for Part-Time Entrepreneurs and Small Businesses

MYLES TAYLOR

Side Hustle Law: 9 Essential Lessons for Part-Time Entrepreneurs and Small Businesses by Myles Taylor. Published by Myles Taylor and RHTWorks Media in Sacramento, California.

www.SideHustleLawBook.com

First edition.

ISBN-13: 978-1-79-403759-5

This book is for general information and educational purposes only. The characters referred to in this book are fictional. There is no warranty regarding any of the information provided in this book. Nothing in this book constitutes legal advice, nor does it create any attorney-client relationship. The law is fact and location specific and is always changing, and legal advice is dependent on individual circumstances. Consult with an attorney in your jurisdiction if you have legal questions.

TABLE OF CONTENTS

"In the early stage of a business—you can't break the law, but you kind of have to break the rules a little bit."

Peter Rahal, founder of RXBAR
("How I Built This" Podcast, 2018).

INTRODUCTION

It was the year 1989, and Brian needed a way to pay for college. He had dropped out of high school and had a poor academic record. Fortunately, he found a loophole and enrolled at a well-respected Canadian university. The problem was figuring out how to afford the tuition.

Brian bought a truck for $700, printed some flyers, and started a side hustle: hauling people's junk. He picked up old furniture, magazine collections, broken furnaces, and more. He would come to people's homes and charge to take it all to the dump. After knocking on doors and searching for clients, it was an article in his local paper that helped him get his first real influx of work. After eight years, he was generating a million dollars a year running a business picking up unwanted things.

Brian's company was 1-800-GOT-JUNK. Today, it is an international company doing over $300 million in annual revenue, and Brian Scudamore is a very wealthy person. What began as a college side hustle with a simple idea turned into a massive and extraordinary success. Whether you have your sights on creating the next golden venture, or whether you just want extra money in your pocket, you see the opportunity to make it happen.

But in the meantime, you are thinking about your job. The job that you may love some days but hate on others. The job that you may feel you have little control over or no upward future in. The job that, for better or worse, you may feel won't last forever. Your job isn't everything, and it isn't the only way to make money.

You have an idea now. It might be small at first, but it feels promising. It could bring happiness to someone. It could solve someone's problem. It is something that a stranger might buy. Your idea can become a business, or it might already be one. You have had long talks about it with friends. You have prepared a business plan. You have plunged in headfirst.

You know there are many risks. People might hate what you are selling. They might not see the value. Someone else might have done it better than you. That is why you are looking to build up your business skills and knowledge, since that will help you minimize risk and identify more opportunities. You pick up sales and marketing to avoid folding based on lack of exposure and revenue. You learn operation techniques to streamline your processes to make every dollar generated go further. You read about bookkeeping to put your numbers in order.

There are also pitfalls arising from legal issues. Like your physician, a good lawyer can help you with preventative legal work. They can help you plan and protect yourself. They can help advise you on legal risks and help get your papers in order, so if something bad does happen, you will not be facing a complete unknown or total loss. That's where this book comes in. This book is the "diet and exercise" advice that your business needs to help it stay healthy and strong and to assist you in making better decisions as you move forward.

SCOPE OF THIS BOOK

We want to have a clear foundation about what a side hustle is and what type of side hustle on which we are going to focus. A side hustle is a business you work on outside of your normal day job. Some people use them as a way to fulfill their entrepreneurial desires. Some people use them as a way to work toward financial independence or to save for retirement. Some people are driven by a passion or creative impulse.

TYPES OF SIDE HUSTLES

In a sense, there are two types of side hustles. There are those where you are simply trying to generate some extra cash. This might be accomplished by participating in the sharing economy as an Uber or Lyft driver, an Airbnb host, or even completing online surveys to get some pocket change. On the other hand, there are side hustles that exist as full-fledged businesses with the only caveat being that you split your time between it and some other activities. This book is intended for those entrepreneurs that fall into the second category.

Within that group, side hustles still come in a variety of forms. There are services, like doing bicycle repairs, being a consultant, or offering résumé editing. There are products, such as selling handmade crafts, mobile apps, or t-shirts. There are social media and affiliate opportunities. There are blogs, vlogs, and other media. There are subscription boxes. There are crafts, teaching, consulting, and more. They can be passive income sources or active ones. Any business can be (or start as) a side hustle.

Side hustles might include ideas related to your full-time gig. For example, a chef might start selling a new protein bar, or a marketing professional might make a website with branded content. However, there are plenty of side hustles that have nothing to do with one's day job. An automotive technician might have a great idea for an improved shower cap, or a kindergarten teacher could create a home security device. While there is some advantage for people that already know an industry to continue operating in it on the side, there is nothing stopping you from exploring other fields.

THE ENTREPRENEURIAL ITCH

If you haven't noticed, side hustles are everywhere. Everyone is either starting a business or dreaming about it. From the thousands of YouTube videos to the podcasts, blogs, and references in print media, side hustles and startups have exploded. The concept is nothing new, but a confluence of several factors have contributed to the phenomenon.

One reason for side hustle popularity is the interest in startup and business-focused media. There is no doubt that some level of feedback loop has been generated. Hearing these success stories and learning about businesses through TV shows, podcasts, and blogs have created a demand for content that then inspires even more people to take the plunge into entrepreneurship. It's no wonder that we all are craving this and wanting a piece.

Additionally, there is more access than ever before to powerful and affordable tools that can be used to start a business. It comes largely as a result of the Web 2.0 phenomenon of the mid to late 2000s and the speed and availability of the internet. This is especially true for those projects that could not have existed as a side business in the past or would be too cost prohibitive. The internet has demolished the barrier to entry and given everyone the tools to enter the market and compete for consumer dollars. This is especially true for an online business with platforms like Squarespace and Shopify and for mobile app development with the iOS and Google Play stores.

Another major reason for the side hustle boom is financial security, or more appropriately, financial insecurity. Either you lived through the lingering economic blowback from 2008 and struggled to find a job, or you've seen the lasting impact on others. Side hustles grant some control over your future that a day job does not. While you cannot control the market and you cannot force a demand for your products, you might have more control over your future by starting a business when compared with being an employee at someone else's company. You can also bring in the extra income to build a strong emergency fund, pay down debt, and save for retirement. In early 2018, a survey of nearly 1000, Americans working on side hustles found that 65.9% of the respondents were primarily motivated in their business to get access to more spending money. The next two most popular motivations were increasing savings and paying off debt. With the oppression of high university tuition, high housing costs, and well-documented wage stagnation, there is no question that building yourself multiple revenue streams is going to do some good.

The legal lessons addressed here apply to any business, but especially for those that one day want to scale it into a full-time opportunity. Whether it's an infant startup of the next great tech company, or whether it is a passion project selling crafts, you need to be informed about the world you have entered.

WHAT THIS BOOK COVERS

This book will teach you a few of the basic legal concepts that a new small business or side hustle might encounter. It will take you from first considering the idea, how to get to the point of putting something on the market, and eventually hiring some help to assist you in growing the business. While there are many concepts that you will need to learn when starting up a new venture, the law is one aspect of a business that is often ignored by owners in the early days. The law impacts what you can and cannot do in your business. It impacts what happens once you start to accumulate sales, make some money, and grow.

This book intends to teach you some legal lessons in a compact, efficient manner. Every dollar counts, especially at the early stages. You may not have the money for a fancy website or to hire someone to develop sales strategies. You might not be able to afford a bookkeeper yet. An expensive business lawyer could be out of reach for your budget. But just because you can't yet afford to hire someone with specialized knowledge, it does not make the law any less important.

Even if you are starting a side hustle with the goals of just supplementing some personal income or pursuing a passion project, the same rules and regulations will apply to you that will apply to someone starting a full-time business. While you may not be a major fish for lawsuits and government regulators now, you never know what will happen in the future. You could get randomly picked from a list for a tax audit or you could grow large enough that you get specifically targeted for a health and safety inspection. You might make a competitor or customer so angry they submit an anonymous complaint. The legal implications of your business are there whether you like it or not, and the high price of legal advice does not mean you can afford to neglect it entirely.

With all that said, there are some things this book is not meant to address. First, this book does not replace the advice of a lawyer. This book covers general concepts in a very cursory fashion. Each one of these topics could be a full course in law school and still not cover it all. As you start to get a taste of it from this book, the law and its application are complicated, multifaceted, and fact specific.

This is not just a throwaway statement that lawyers say to be difficult. This book cannot address all the facts that one faces or laws that apply. Hopefully, however, it gives you enough basic knowledge to save you some time when you do need to see a lawyer by having a more productive dialogue. The law has its own language, so getting some Law 101 will help you speak more fluently with your lawyer. Since business lawyers typically charge by the hour, having more efficient conversations translates directly into saving you money.

Next, this book addresses principles and situations with a focus on United States legal and business environments and, in some instances, specifically uses California as the example. The general concepts will carry across the world, but both law and business customs can be geographically specific.

Finally, this book is not exhaustive. There are many more legal concepts that are applicable to businesses. For sake of keeping this book simple and direct, we are focusing on only a handful. As you are starting and growing a business, you already have your hands full and there is no sense in overburdening you in just one sitting.

WHAT IS "THE LAW"?

Although this is a towering philosophic question, we can keep with the theme and provide a basic primer on "the law" to lay a foundation for the lessons in this book. In the United States, following the common law traditions of England, the law comes from a variety of sources. There is no single book or compilation of all laws. In many instances, it isn't as simple as wondering whether something is legal and plugging it into a search engine. This is not only because of the multiple sources of law but also because the facts of any circumstance are crucial to interpreting whether and how a particular law or legal concept applies.

SOURCES OF LAW

In general, there is legislature-made law and judge-made law. There are also laws created by municipalities like cities, and there are more specific regulations created by executive agencies.

At the top of the pyramid is the United States Constitution. This is the founding legal document that is the self-declared supreme law of the land. Among other things, Article I of the Constitution grants Congress certain powers to write law. Congress creates and passes federal statutes. Those statutes might directly allow or restrict something, or they might enable an executive agency to write regulations to carry out the statute's purpose. The Constitution further lays out the general rules for the President and the executive branch in Article II and the United States Supreme Court in Article III.

After the federal government, each state has its own constitution. The state legislatures also pass statutes and grant executive agency authority to create regulations. These laws cannot loosen federal restrictions, but they can build on the requirements. For example, a number of states have decriminalized or even legalized recreational cannabis use. This does not change the fact that it remains illegal under federal law, but it means that state attorneys general and local district attorneys are not going to prosecute. On the other hand, most states and have passed laws more strictly regulating matters like minimum wage than at the federal level, requiring employees be paid even more than the federal minimum.

There are also municipal laws. County boards of supervisors and city councils pass ordinances regulating matters like property zoning, building codes, and health and safety. Since municipalities are smaller in size, their ordinances manifest local sentiment, which can vary significantly.

Beyond the legislated rules at the various levels, there is judge-made law—that is, court decisions that interpret and apply statutes and "common law" principles. This is done by the courts of appeal, who hear cases after a trial court has ruled on a dispute. The decisions from those appellate courts become precedent that will be followed by other courts. There are multiple levels of appellate courts in the state and federal systems, including the United States Supreme Court, which is the ultimate judicial body responsible for well-known cases like *Brown v. Board of Education*, *Roe v. Wade*, or *Citizens United v. FEC*.

In addition to actual law, there are non-government sources for rules. These include private rules, such as the policies at a local flea market, the restrictions provided by a homeowners association, or the terms for using a website. There are also norms and industry standards that are deeply ingrained such that they might as well carry a legal penalty for violating.

This basic overview and background will provide you with some context for addressing the lessons covered in this book. Understanding the sources of law not only gives you an appreciation for the complexity but also shows how you need to be mindful that rules will change depending on where you operate.

CHARACTERS FOR THE BOOK

Because the application of law is fact specific, we need some examples to draw from while we cover the lessons in this book. In America, law students spend most of their time reading court cases, understanding the facts and circumstances the court was facing, and using them to explain and appreciate the fundamental legal concepts they study. In practice, we find that even similar situations that one lawyer may have encountered a dozen times before can still have factual nuances that change the game for the client. As both a means of education and illustration, we will introduce four different people in the beginning stages of their businesses.

First, there is Sara. She works in the medical field and is on her feet all day. Sara enjoys her career and sees opportunity for growth, but she has a passion for business and a drive to be creative that isn't being fulfilled at the hospital. As a lifelong artist, she has been developing a series of colorful children's characters that she plans to turn into plush toys and animated stories. Sara has considered partnering with her friend, Kurt, who she says is great at making websites and has his own successful e-commerce store.

Second, there is Luis. He is entering his senior year at a local university. Luis spent his childhood making homemade taffy with his mother, and he recently started making it again for his friends. He incorporates interesting and less traditional flavor combinations that are not found in most stores. Luis has decided to start selling the taffy, and he used a college class assignment to write a business plan as the springboard for his project. While he thinks he will land a job after graduation, he's nervous about his student loans and wants to get a head start on them.

Next, there is Alex. He is a trained dancer. To pay the bills, he works at city hall as a clerk. He has given sporadic dance classes before, but he has not had a dedicated space to make it worthwhile to really pursue. However, Alex's friend recently opened a yoga studio and has offered to rent out time slots to allow him to teach dance regularly and to afford him the opportunity to open a real dance school. He is interested in turning it into a sustainable side business and putting some of his lessons down into a program he could sell to future students.

Finally, there is Myra. She is a computer programmer. Myra's work hours are inconsistent and project based. Some weeks she has a lot of down time, while in others, she is incredibly busy. Myra loves cooking and has projects around that passion. She has a vlog and is starting to get tons of views on her channel. The opportunity she really sees is to start a recipe club and meal planning mobile app that integrates with her cooking videos. Myra was also discussing with her uncle, who is a successful business owner, investing some money into Myra's venture.

We will follow these four and get to know their businesses better as we work through the lessons in this book. You will see as they face decisions and enter new stages while navigating the law as entrepreneurs.

LESSON 1

DON'T VIOLATE YOUR EXISTING EMPLOYMENT TERMS

If you are like most people starting a side hustle, you have a day job. It is by no means required, but the "side" in side hustle implies there is something else on which you spend the majority of your time. This does not have to be a job, as you might be a parent, a student, or an owner of another business. However, if you do have a day job, you need to keep your employer in mind when starting up.

YOUR EMPLOYER'S POLICIES

If you are working while starting your side business, there could be risk to both your job and your side business. It largely depends on the policies your employer has and any agreements you may have signed. You need to look out for and brush up on any employment agreements or policies that you are subject to before you get going.

In most places, the default status for your employment is "at will." This means you can leave your job whenever you want, but it also means you can be fired whenever your boss wants. There are some circumstances and reasons that are protected, such as if you recently made a complaint about your wage statement or are about to take parental leave, and you can't be fired due to your race, religion, sex, and other protected bases. Yet, outside of the limited exceptions, an "at will" employee can be fired for any other reason or for no reason at all. It could be because you wore orange shoes on Tuesday. It could be for making a popcorn and fish casserole in the breakroom microwave. It could also be for moonlighting at another company or starting a side business.

To reduce the chances of impacting your job, you will want to check your employee handbook and any policies provided to you by your employer. If there is a specific policy, you will have some insight on how they feel about the subject. At larger companies, the human resources department should be prepared to tell you how the company handles this. The benefit of having a specific policy is that you can consult it to determine where the line is. Your boss might have a policy that you cannot enter other employment that impacts your present job or that is in the same field. Knowing this ahead of time can help steer your priorities and hopefully avoid spending tons of time on a side project that you later find is going to get you into trouble.

At smaller companies, it is less likely you will have a specific policy about outside employment or side projects. You then have some choices to make. You could contact someone in charge and ask, but this may not feel feasible. You may not want to put your employer on notice that you will be using your free time on another venture because you are worried they will consider this at your next review and question your loyalty or dedication. If that is a concern, you can consider strategically asking someone in human resources, who isn't a direct supervisor, about the company's general position on the topic without precisely indicating that you've already made up your mind to start a business.

Your other option is to do nothing and keep it to yourself. The risk you run here is making your boss upset or feel like you have deceived them if they find out later. If your project is in the same industry as your employer, they might feel threatened when they find out on their own. You should be aware that bringing the project to your boss' attention could go well or poorly depending on the personalities involved. There is no protected legal right to work multiple jobs or start a business, so this could be a valid basis to terminate you.

We have been discussing "at will" employees generally, but some people operate under employment contracts. If you have an employment contract, it can directly limit what other business activities you can engage in, and there are larger implications than just getting fired. An employment contract, at a minimum, will spell out terms about compensation and duration. There could be a host of other terms, such as work performance expectations, confidentiality, work-for-hire, intellectual property assignment, or exclusivity. You could also be subject to some of these restrictions, even if you are not working under an employment contract.

CONFIDENTIAL INFORMATION

It is common in certain industries for employees to sign confidentiality agreements and notices. If your job involves access to information that needs to be kept secret with your employer, then you cannot use that knowledge in your business on your own time.

Some industries will keep the projects they work on confidential to avoid market competition. For example, in the entertainment and technology worlds, companies keep their lips sealed about new movies, games, gadgets, or other projects until it becomes time to reveal to the public. If information leaks out early, then knockoffs and spoilers can destroy the market potential. In other industries like medicine or finance, companies will not only have internal confidentiality rules to protect their competitive edge, but they also are subject to laws over their clients' privacy. Violations can be devastating and subject the company to fines and penalties as well as public backlash, so these companies should be taking protection of the sensitive information especially seriously. If any of these situations apply, you need to be aware of what information you can use and what information belongs to someone else.

Additionally, confidentiality is used to keep the proprietary information under wraps so others cannot benefit from it. In 2014, Facebook spent $2 billion to acquire Oculus, a company best known for its virtual reality headset, the Oculus Rift. Just a year later, a company called ZeniMax sued Oculus, alleging the founder had been hired years before to build a head-mounted display prototype. That prototype was claimed to have been developed for ZeniMax and then ultimately used to create the Oculus Rift. ZeniMax asserted that Oculus' founder had signed a confidentiality agreement and then breached it by using part of the computer code in his new project. After a couple of years of litigation, a jury awarded ZeniMax $500 million in damages for breaching confidentially.

While your business is not likely to face this fate, the improper use of confidential information is a problem that can linger as your business grows. It's key that you appreciate the fact that everything you know and have access to as a result of your day job is not free range for use in your business.

WORK-FOR-HIRE AND ASSIGNMENTS

When you start your business, you may be initially thinking about it while at work or in class. You are dreaming about the possibilities, what you would do with that extra cash you'll make, or how you will handle problems you anticipate having to solve. While thinking is okay, you need to be careful about doing any concrete activities in support of your business while on your employer's time or using any of your employer's resources.

There is a legal concept called work-for-hire. This is an issue in copyright law, which is discussed more later on this book. You'll want to ensure what you work on is owed by you, and not your employer. At its core, work-for-hire is a doctrine that gives an employer ownership over work that is produced for them.

This makes sense and is necessary in most business contexts. If you're a writer for a news site, your employer pays you to write articles for them to publish. If you're a designer, your employer pays you to create new packaging for its clients. It makes sense that what you prepare at work would be owned by your employer—isn't that they're paying you for?

For current matter, the courts apply the test in the Copyright Act of 1976. The act defines a "work made for hire" as: (1) a work prepared by an employee within the scope of his or her employment; or (2) a work specially ordered or commissioned, in certain circumstances.

So what is something within your scope of employment? There are many court decisions that have tried to figure that out. An examining court would consider factors including:

- Did the hired person need special skills to prepare the work?
- Did the tools used come from the hiring business, or were they owned by the hired person?
- Where was the work performed?
- How long has the relationship between the parties lasted?
- Did the hired person assign rights to other projects they worked on to the hiring business?

- What type of discretion did the hiring business have over the work?
- How was the hired person paid?

These factors get weighed against each other in the specific situation to determine whether the work is going to belong to the hiring business or the hired person.

An example of the work-for-hire concept came about in 2009. The heirs of famous comic book artist Jack Kirby attempted to claim the rights to dozens of comic books published between 1958 and 1963 that had introduced the world to memorable characters like the Avengers, Incredible Hulk, X-Men, Spider-Man and more. Marvel Comics, in turn, asserted that the comics were covered under the work-for-hire doctrine. The federal court hearing the case sided with Marvel, finding it owned the rights to the characters Jack Kirby has created. The heirs walked away with nothing, and Marvel went on to create an unparalleled series of blockbuster movies.

The work-for-hire concept doesn't just exist for employer-employee situations. If you do freelance work, there are instances where the work you do might be owned by a client as a matter of law. This largely depends on the deliverable itself. The requirements include that the work was specifically ordered, there is a written contract stating it is work-for-hire, and the work falls into one of the work-for-hire categories. The categories include helping with a collective work, a movie, a translation, a supplementary work, a compilation, instructional text, test materials, and more.

A concept related to work-for-hire is the intellectual property assignment. As part of your work, you may have signed some agreement to transfer the rights in any created works to the company that is paying you. This type of assignment is common for companies that have people preparing creative works for them. The worker will sign some document assigning the rights to the work product. Since your labor is being paid for, the company paying you wants to own whatever it is you create. By assigning the rights to the work you have done, this would fill in any gap left from the work-for-hire doctrine and non-employee workers.

While there may not be any policy at your job that would outright restrict you from working on a side hustle, you need to ensure that your business remains entirely yours. This is especially the case if your job is in an industry that overlaps with your business as there is a risk that your employer could try to claim rights to what you develop. If you have signed any confidentiality notice or non-disclosure agreement, this is further compounded. By using confidential information or working on your business while at your job, you run the risk that your employer could claim ownership in your ideas, seek a court order to block you from operating, or even sue you to recover the profits you generated. Not good.

The question of ownership over what you develop is not only limited to workers in private companies. At least since 1980 with the passage of the Bayh-Dole Act, universities have systematically asserted rights to research and development activities that occur on campus. These policies vary from university to university, but if you are a student working on research at a university, you must be aware of the scope of what the school may own.

The monolith internet company Google began while co-founders Larry Paige and Sergey Brin were graduate students at Stanford University. It was during their work at Stanford that they developed the technology that became Google's famous PageRank algorithm. PageRank was the proprietary way Google has managed to provide such useful search results and shape the internet as we know it. Although Larry and Sergey were the developers, Stanford asserted ownership over the PageRank patent because Larry and Sergey were students working on research with the university when it came about. Early in the company's life, Google had to give 1.8 million shares to Stanford for a license to use the technology. When Google had its initial public offering in 2004, Stanford sold a majority of its shares and banked around $330 million. Quite the return on its *non*-investment.

Having a day job or being a student does not mean your business is doomed to have someone else claim they own it, nor do you always need to be afraid that your night and weekend business will get you fired. Instead, you can sidestep these issues by being conscious of the laws affecting you. Read your employee handbook, check with the human resources department, and look for any policies about work-for-hire. If you spend a little time becoming informed, then you can plan and act to protect yourself.

CHARACTER EXAMPLE

To help understand these concepts, let's look at Myra's situation. She is working on an app to deliver recipes and meal planning to compliment her vlog. She also works on projects where her employer is hired by a client to develop software, including mobile apps. As part of an arrangement like that, the employer likely will have included a term to assign the rights in anything the employees work on that is connected to the job. The employer would have policies and agreements in place stating that all the computer code written and ideas developed in the process will not be owned by the employee.

So what happens if Myra starts working on her own app while at work? In some instances, her employer might gain some rights to her personal project. One factor to look at is whether Myra used her employer's resources or worked on her app while at the office. If she is using the laptop that her boss has provided for her job, even while at home, that will be considered. If she is working on the app while on the clock and using her employer's Wi-Fi and printer, then these facts would hurt her. We also can't avoid that Myra works as a computer programmer and app developer at her job, which is in part the same skills that she uses for her recipe and meal planning app. At the same time, maybe Myra has not signed any documents about assigning the rights in what she creates to her employer, or maybe her employer has expressly permitted outside projects but only under certain terms. There are many items to consider.

This sort of factor-based test doesn't provide clean answers; instead, you want to use it to plan. No single fact is going to change whether your work belongs to you or someone else. Instead, the best practice would be to steer clear of the factors that might deem a project as property of her employer. If Myra pulls up her side business email while on a computer at work, it does not automatically change anything. However, she would be advised to keep her day job separate from her business as much as possible to prevent any questions from coming up.

Further, if Myra has signed a non-disclosure agreement with her job or is privy to proprietary information, she must be careful about how she uses the knowledge she has obtained. Let's say the new project at her job is working on an interactive magazine app for a large cooking enterprise. While at work, Myra learns about a new trend that would be pushed next year for marshmallow-coated everything. It isn't public yet, but it's going to be the subject of a major marketing plan, as the client has a bunch of new products they are preparing to launch. She thinks it's weird—marshmallows everywhere? But with that knowledge, she decides to add a new feature to her own app to aggregate marshmallow recipes, deals on marshmallow products, and add content about the upcoming trend.

On the one hand, this seems innocent. Myra isn't taking any business away from the client, so why does it matter? The problem here is the confidential information. Myra has acted to improve her side hustle, using information that she obtained only by virtue of her job. It is not a matter of public knowledge that this big company will be pushing marshmallows next season. The only way Myra learned this was by virtue of her relationship as an employee at her job, and moreover, she has signed a confidentiality agreement.

There are legal and practical implications to this example. For one, Myra could be fired. She has breached policies of her employer, and she did it for financial gain. Additionally, Myra has negatively impacted her employer. If the client found out that there are information leaks, the client would likely take their business elsewhere. That would put the sights on Myra for having cost her employer money. Depending on how sensitive the information was, the client might even file a claim against Myra and her business, including seeking a court order to prevent her from acting.

While Myra's marshmallow feature is not going to see backlash like massive technology deals of Oculus and Google, she needs to appreciate potential problems and remain mindful of any restrictions on the information obtained through her day job. The bigger the wall one can build between a day job and side business, the lesser the chance there will be an issue in the future.

Lesson 1 Takeaways...

✓ Check with your employer's policies about starting a business on the side.

✓ Use care to avoid working on your business while at work or using your employer's resources.

✓ If you have an employment contract or other agreement, review the terms and ensure you stay in compliance. This includes assigning the rights to the work product and keeping information confidential.

LESSON 2

OBTAIN THE NECESSARY LICENSES AND PERMITS TO OPERATE LAWFULLY

Your business has an impact beyond just you. It not only affects your employer, but it also affects your customers, competition, and the public. Since you do not operate in a bubble, the government has a vested interest in ensuring that businesses behave within certain parameters. The federal government, the various states, and all counties and cities regulate business activities in different ways. This often takes the form of licenses and permits.

One of the primary interactions between a business and the government relates to collecting taxes. Business sales tax revenues are one of the sources of state and local government revenue in the United States. There are no federal sales taxes, and except for Alaska, Delaware, Montana, New

Hampshire and Oregon, all other states impose some form of sales taxes. Cities and counties also impose their own sales taxes on top. Business activities are also regulated for health and safety reasons, and you may need occupational licensing, permits from the fire and police departments, building permits, and more.

BUSINESS LICENSE

Anytime you operate in a commercial context, you need a general business license. These are provided by the state, county, or city in which you plan to operate. The business license is meant to register and identify your business activity, protect the public, and ensure the city or county can collect taxes from you. Anyone who wants to regularly conduct business will be subject to the requirement of holding a valid business license.

Further, a general business license is not only needed where your headquarters is located. If you are conducting business outside your home base, you will technically need a business license from each location. If you are selling goods, you also need a seller's permit. If you grow a business to the point where you operate in multiple jurisdictions, then you will need a business license for each. This ends up affecting mobile businesses as well, such as craftspersons or antique dealers that attend farmers markets and fairs in multiple areas. It can be a hassle to comply if every town wants to see their own stamped permit before you can put up your tent at the farmers market. While it is unlikely that the city will have an inspector checking every booth at these events, the organizers may bar you from participating without licensing proof.

TYPES OF REGULATED ACTIVITIES

Beyond a general business license, specific types of businesses also have license requirements. If you look hard enough, you are bound to find some laws governing your actual business activities.

Some types of business are notorious for having hosts of regulations. A business that does anything with food or beverages will have multiple levels of regulation. Products like tobacco and alcohol are controlled even more. If you sell or use chemicals or materials that could cause harm (even liquid nitrogen!), then you will have to comply with rules involving the handling of hazardous substances.

It isn't just goods that face extra regulation; services get hit just as hard. Cosmetology is an area that is surprisingly strict in its rules and barrier to entry, including many hours of classroom training and tests. Massage and other services that involve interacting with people physically typically require licenses. Even hauling trash, acting as a handyman, and performing yard care and lawn mowing can require permits. Many people object to what are seen as overly restrictive licensure requirements that make it harder for people to start businesses. Of course, those that promulgate the rules claim they are protecting the public and ensuring a minimum quality guarantee. Whether you like it or not, these laws exist at present, and you can't get around them all.

Before you start, you will want to check with your county and city. There is usually an office dedicated to handling business and other permitted activities. The Small Business Administration also has online and in-person resources across the country that can help point you in the right direction. Although there are tons of rules, there are some easy-to-use guides out there to help get you started.

PROBLEMS WITH VIOLATING

Licenses and permits allow you to operate legitimately in the eyes of the government. Can you just ignore licenses and permits? Sure—until you get caught. Operating a business without proper licensing can be a criminal offense punishable by both fines and jail time.

The most obvious issue with ignoring these requirements is the threat that the government could shut you down. Imagine the horror of having a health department official arrive at your door and bar you from completing a major cupcake order that you need to pay the rent for the month. This is a legitimate fear, and if you are struggling, it could be a death sentence for your business to get unexpectedly hit like this. It may be unlikely that you face harsh penalties at first, but the risk is still out there. You can ignore the speed limit while driving too, but then you will be constantly looking over your shoulder, increasing the risk of accident, and having a near-heart attack when you see a black and white car with a roof rack.

Running any business, large or small, has tons of risks. Are you going to get sales? Are there printing errors? Will it ship on time? Did the website malfunction? Is your employee late? You are going to be worrying all the time. You should try to reduce some of the worries that are within your power and spend your time stressing over parts of the business that will help it grow and progress.

EXAMPLE: HANDYMAN SERVICES

Let's take handyman services as an example. People with the skills to handle odd jobs around the house can be in hot demand. This would include hanging pictures, fixing cabinet doors, replacing locks, or other general maintenance and repair work. In California, you can perform unlicensed handyman services if the total value of your work is under $500. If you go beyond this, you will need a license.

What happens if your client asks you to go beyond the scope of a handyman and wants your help painting their house, rewriting an outlet, or fixing the plumbing? Maybe you've done this to your own house, taken a course on it, or worked on tasks like this at your job. Seems like no big deal. However, this falls into contractor work, and the law imposes harsh penalties against unlicensed contractors. For a first offense in California, it is possible to see a minor jail sentence, a fine of $5,000, and other administrative penalties that range from a few hundred to several thousand dollars. If you get caught again, the penalties and fines can increase. There are also non-criminal claims that can be brought against you by the client to pull back all the money they paid you in the first place to leave you empty handed.

EXAMPLE: FOOD PREPARATION

Another example is food preparation. The problem with a home kitchen, assuming it is allowed, is both practical and legal. Practically speaking, if you get enough orders, you're not going to have the space and equipment you really need for the large batches or continuous production as your business demands. The convenience of cooking at home, and the reduced expense, are very significant factors at first, but there are reasons that larger scale businesses aren't run out of the home.

In California, the Legislature passed the Cottage Food Operations bill in 2012. The Cottage Food Operations bill dramatically lowered the barrier to entry for smaller operations and supported more vendors starting out. This bill provided rules for certain homemade food products sold on relatively smaller scales with specific rules and limits to follow. For example, using a kitchen where dogs, cats, or other pets are able to enter could knock you out of eligibility. There were also rules requiring that the location of your kitchen (a.k.a. your house address) be printed on the packaging. This law only permitted preparing foods that had lower risks of foodborne illness, like baked goods or dry items, and it capped the amount of money you could earn before you were required to switch to a professional kitchen environment.

The problem for a side hustler is that you likely don't have the time to be operating a full-scale location while holding down your day job. If you can't swing leasing a space for your own professional kitchen, then your products are usually going to be created in private, commercial kitchens once your business gets to a certain size. A commercial kitchen is a kitchen that you can pay, usually by the hour, to use and operate. Catering companies will often rent out commercial kitchen space when they need to prepare food for an event, since the cost of building and maintaining a kitchen that only is used on weekends or sporadic events would be inefficient and a waste of money. One of the big advantages to using a commercial kitchen is that it should be easier to comply with the various health and safety laws regulating you. You may also get access to professional-level appliances and a bigger workspace that will help you with working at higher volumes. The downside is the cost, but you will have added expenses like this once you reach that level.

EXAMPLE: CHILD CARE

To operate any child care facility, whether full-time or part-time, you need a state license. This refers to any infant care, pre-school, or extended day care that provides non-medical, supervised care of children. In California, the Department of Social Services issues the licenses and divides child care activities between family care and child care centers. The former is operated from your house, while the latter is operated from an outside location.

In addition to the state license, you will likely need a special use permit for the location, clearance from the fire marshal, criminal background checks, and an inspection to show that you have sufficient supplies and equipment. Finally, you have to grapple with zoning, which leads us to the next topic.

ZONING

There are rules not only about what you do but also where you do it. This is called zoning. Counties and cities enact zoning laws to divide up their maps and allow for certain activities to occur in certain places. People with houses usually don't want large factories and liquor stores next door, as it impacts property values, creates noise, and hurts the neighborhood feel. So there are local pushes to put the various things we do into neat, color-coded sections on the map. The basic classifications in zoning are residential, commercial, industrial, mixed use, and special project areas, and each can then be broken down further into various levels and densities.

At first, your business may be operated out of your garage or bedroom. Just look at Apple Computer or any number of tech startups. Working in a garage or a dorm while donning a hoodie and holding a bowl of instant ramen noodles is almost like a rite of passage for those companies. Many small businesses start this way, and some never find the need to change. This could be because it is a solo operation, entirely web based, or not large enough to warrant its own separate location.

If you are operating out of your home, you need to be aware that it is likely not zoned for commercial activity. If someone makes a complaint based on too many noisy 4:00 AM deliveries in your driveway, or that you're having too many visitors to your apartment to help bejewel all those handbags, you can get on someone's radar and may receive contact from your local enforcement agency. If you are renting, then it could also be a landlord issue, so check your lease to make sure you aren't in breach and risking an eviction.

Until you can afford to rent space that is properly zoned, you will want to keep your physical operations quiet and nonintrusive for neighbors. This will better your chances of growing your business and saving on overhead for the time being. If you do encounter issues, look at co-working spaces or subleasing a small amount of space from another business through a commercial broker, as these will lessen the hassle and cost of finding your own space outright.

CHARACTER EXAMPLE

Alex, the dance instructor, is offering classes out of his friend's yoga studio. He is thrilled to finally have a location, but he is concerned about doing this right, especially being a city employee. First, he will need a business license. Alex needs to ensure that the business is operating legally in the eyes of the government and collecting any taxes he will owe for it. Alex has instructional materials and music that is displayed for sale at every class, which generates additional revenue for the business. Since he is selling a good at the location, he will need to apply for a seller's permit and collect sales tax. As a dance instructor, there may not be a specific permit required, but it is still important to check. Some occupations you would never expect can require special licenses such as fortune tellers, beekeepers, and movie projector operators.

Luis, the college student, is making and selling his homemade taffy. As shown, food products are heavily regulated down to the local level. There are laws that govern packaging, ingredients, storage and more, but where he can manufacture and store his candy will be especially important.

Luis learned his recipe from his family, and he's developed his current taffy through tinkering at home in his apartment kitchen. At first, this might work great. He's already paying rent, and the kitchen is sufficient for Luis to prepare small batches of taffy. Yet, as Luis' business grows, he needs to evaluate other options. His roommate is also becoming tired of the mess and the noise—the free taffy from the test batches is only going to get him so far. Luis could explore using a co-packer, which is a business that will manufacture your food product based on ingredients and specifications you provide them. Even more so than with a commercial kitchen, using a co-packer means he won't need to worry as much about health and safety inspections involved in manufacturing, since he wouldn't be doing the actual manufacturing himself. A co-packer would provide convenience too, because he won't need to spend the time making the food himself. This comes with the loss of absolute control over the process and the cost of paying the co-packer, but it may be worth it.

Rather than trying to hide from the government just to save the few bucks it takes to acquire a license, you may be better served thinking of the government as your begrudging silent partner. That partner has given you access to roads to make deliveries on, a neighborhood desirable enough to have consistent foot traffic, and a venue for resolving disputes in court. Your silent partner has set up a relatively predictable system where you don't legitimately fear every day that some madman is going walk in your office and steal your company and all its assets from you. In exchange, the silent partner generally has some influence over how you run things (regulations) and wants a cut of what you generate (taxes).

Will this make you feel any better when it comes time to wade into the bureaucracy or pay for another permit? Probably not. But since there is no real escaping the government, you can try and have a positive outlook.

Lesson 2 Takeaways...

- ✓ The government regulates businesses at all levels, including local taxation, health, and safety.

- ✓ Check for licenses or permits needed for your type of business through your state, county, and city websites.

- ✓ Try to make peace with the government as your begrudging silent partner.

LESSON 3

IF YOU WANT A BUSINESS PARTNER, PLAN APPROPRIATELY

Starting a business is intimidating. In theory, you might be more comfortable having a knowledgeable friend or trusted colleague hold your hand while you plunge into the deep end. Yet, starting with or later obtaining a business partner comes with a host of potential legal and personal problems that can tank a money-making operation. Proper planning is essential to avoid those pitfalls.

PARTNER ADVANTAGES

A partner, in a general sense, would be someone that has ownership in the business with you. There is a specific legal meaning to the terms "partner" and "partnership," but most people use them to generally refer to someone you go into business with. There are a few reasons why you might join with a partner, and it is important that you identify your reasons before doing anything.

First, you might seek out a partner that has complementary skills. If you are great with product design and operations, but terrible with sales and bookkeeping, you could partner with someone that already has those missing abilities. If you're the mathematician or the engineer, you might pair with an artist or a writer.

Another reason for joining with a partner could be to multiply your effectiveness. You and a partner might be skilled in the same area, but together, you have better chance of success and can work harder because you have two heads looking at problems and understanding the intricacies.

Additionally, a partner might bring much needed financing. We are talking about a business here, and every business needs capital. It could be that you don't expect the partner to work in the business on a day-to-day basis, but you are looking to access investment money and sage wisdom, so you're willing to share in setting of the overall vision, resolving 30,000-foot problems, and ultimately the profits.

By the same token, a partner might reduce risk, or at least the perception of risk, for your business. Having someone on the same level as you to help strategize and make decisions about the company will not only assist with taking some of the work of your shoulders, but it also can motivate you and increase a sense of accountability. While you may not be looking for outside investment today, it could become part of your future. It's worth noting that some investors and venture capitalists prefer businesses with co-founders.

This is not uncommon for tech companies in particular. In the very early days of Instagram— before it was the Instagram you know—founder Kevin Systrom had been talking with a venture capitalist who conditioned an investment on Systrom's finding a co-founder. This caused him to tap his friend Mike Krieger, and the two of them ended up co-founding the company, which then sold to Facebook just fifteen months later for $1 billion. The general thought from investors behind preferring to invest where there is a co-founder that brings some complementary skills and the ability to share and commiserate in the experiences of building a business is that it will lead to a higher chance of success.

There is no doubt that starting a business is an emotional process. Partners can make some of the hardest parts easier. Partners can give you someone to lean on, confide in, and share in both the ups and downs. But like any relationship, partnerships aren't always rosy, and sometimes they end in flames.

PROBLEMS WITH PARTNERS

No matter its size, the backbone of every business is its people. Those people are both the reasons why it can flourish and why it can wilt. Those people have passion, dedication, and creativity, but they will experience frustration, jealousy, and exhaustion. When you add a partner, you are adding someone that will be making decisions with you at the top. A partner is someone with a stake in the game beyond anyone that works for you. This partner will hopefully ease some of the burdens that come from being an entrepreneur, since you have someone that is sharing the grueling experience with you, but it can create havoc when your visions do not align or your communication falls out of sync.

A significant problem for business partners is the respective amount of time and energy spent on the business. If one partner feels they are working harder than the other, then disputes are sure to bubble up. This also can happen where one partner feels their input is not valued as much as it should be. Once the business starts to make some money, the question of fair compensation becomes more of a hot topic. Alternatively, if everything in the business starts going downhill, there can be a propensity to blame the other partner for doing something stupid or omitting something vital.

When considering a partner, it is common to look at friends or family and ask one of them to join you. They stick by you through other rough times, so it is natural to consider them as persons to help you run a business. Plus, you don't need to interview them or worry about getting cheated, since you already know them, right?

Before you jump into it, you must understand that you will fundamentally alter your relationship by going into business with someone. There is a near infinite list of examples of businesses that were started by friends or family that end up crumbling. The fall-out then has the tendency to destroy the entire relationship. Since we have high expectations of our friends and family and have different types of interpersonal relationship with them—compared to those individuals we know through work or other settings—the breakdown after a failed partnership with a friend or family member can result in a permanent loss. But it doesn't have to be this way every time.

PLAN FOR A BUSINESS DIVORCE

Divorces by married couples are the most contentious and heated when they involve children and substantial money or property. All the other fights that come in divorces are there just to sway a division of money, property, or custody. Many people think of their business as their baby, and the whole point of a business is to make money. Like a nasty divorce, there is almost no escaping the fact that a business breakup is going to be tough, but there is still hope.

You don't want to think about it now because the ideas are all flowery and wonderful. You and your potential partner have complementary skills, you have been friends since high school, and you are always there for each other. It seems perfect, but a partnership can implode when you least expect it. When someone else owns part of the business, it means they have a stake in it, even if they stop working day to day. That is the lingering effect of co-ownership, and while it may have motivated you both at first, it now will make separating from each other even harder. If you plan for it, there are legal and practical ways to make a business divorce cleaner.

At the outset, you must spell out everyone's roles in the business early and clearly. Write down all the jobs each of you will each be in charge of and the chain of command for decision making. For example, you may be better at finances and operations, and your partner may be better at sales and product development. If this is the case, give yourselves written department information and scopes of authority. You might also come up with new products or have sales and marketing ideas, but in this hypothetical, your partner gets to be the ultimate decision maker in that area. Then, at some set interval, you can meet up and discuss how the roles are working out and evaluate whether adjustments are needed.

It can seem silly when there are only two of you, but you want an established business structure while things are small and simple and while everyone has a cool head. If you and your partner agree about who is making decisions in certain areas, and that is set forward in a document you can point to later, then the chance of resentment and conflict will be diminished when you are later in a yelling match with very different memories.

You further need open and understood lines of communication. Have a weekly or monthly meeting, phone call, or email between yourselves that briefly discusses any issues that came up since your prior one. You can provide a space to address problems and think of solutions, which doesn't detract from day-to-day business. With whatever you choose, you want to develop a space for your partner and you to raise problems and concerns. Even if there's nothing at a given time, it is the opportunity and the clarity that are important for the business. Sometimes one partner may not be as effective of a communicator of their thoughts and feelings, which can cause them to hold back comments or blurt out complaints in less than productive ways. Establishing a time and place that is safe to bring up concerns it will help to deflate the buildup. The goal of this is to minimize the amount of times you or your partner hold your feelings in or don't feel recognized for hard work. You don't want the balloon to unexpectedly pop.

Next, you should write an agreement with each person's expectations. Partners go into business with expectations that everyone will work hard all the time, but these expectations are not always reality. You and your partner should draft an agreement with at least general work expectations: how many hours, what tasks, and for how long. It should be clear what everyone is doing before you dive into working in the business. Will compensation be related to hours put into the business? Are we going to value the connections or ideas of one partner even if they work less actual hours during the week? What happens if you don't live up to your promises? Are we expecting either partner to invest more of their own money into the business if needed? These are all vital questions to consider and answer.

Additionally, you need an agreement on what will happen if one of you wants to leave the business or dissolve the partnership. Lawyers draft documents called "buy-sell agreements" and "rights of first refusal" for businesses with multiple owners, which bind all owners to rules to handle any attempt to change ownership. A buy-sell or similar type of agreement will require the leaving owner to give the other owners an opportunity to purchase their share in the business before the leaving owner is allowed to offer it for sale to anyone else. It can also be an effective estate planning tool in the event that an owner passes away and their heirs would otherwise then become co-owners. You didn't agree to go into business with your partner's family members, so if your partner passes away, you will want the chance to keep the business control out of the hands of others.

The buy-sell agreement then provides an established method for valuing the business, or it may point to another document like a partnership agreement or corporate bylaws that will provide some language on this. If you have a predefined set of rules on determining how much the business interest is worth, then there is less to fight about in the middle of a breakup. What you think is valuable now is going to be very different when you later feel your business partner has screwed you over.

Defined roles, expectations, and communication should be enshrined in some written form between you and your partner. You should reflect the terms as policy of the company acknowledged by the owners. You need to actually make these policies real too and not a matter of lip service. It's good for you, your partner, and your business in general. No one wants to think about their business breaking down, especially before it has even really started, but you won't have the time to work on this once your business is running at full speed. You will have a million excuses later, and it is unlikely you will get it done. We all know how this goes. If anyone is going to help you grow the business from its infancy, don't procrastinate in considering a predetermined custody arrangement in the event something goes wrong.

CHARACTER EXAMPLE

Sara runs a plushie toy and children's book business that is just starting out. She has been talking to Kurt about joining her as a partner. Sara has known Kurt for years, and they have talked about trying to start a business together before. Kurt's web development skills and knowledge of online marketing provides a strong set of complementary skills for Sara.

Sara already has her business going, but she will admit she's only sold a few toys so far. She does not have much internet presence at the moment, which is where she is sure that the market for her product exists. The animations she is planning for the characters will also require a command of creating online content and spreading it. Sara wants Kurt to join her so she can capitalize on his complementary talents.

Rather than jump into it, Sara should have some informal discussions with Kurt. He is working on a few projects at the moment. Kurt does outside website design and consulting work from home, which Sara needs to consider because it will divide his attention. If there's an important issue that comes up, is Kurt going to drop everything to come to address it? They need to think through what commitments they will make to each other and the business.

Once he is on board, the two should specifically go over the important partnership questions we addressed above. If Sara and Kurt clearly define how much time they'll spend on the business, how and when compensation will be paid out, what percent of ownership Kurt will buy into, what he will give to the business in exchange for it, and what their specific roles in the business will be, then they have a much better chance of avoiding some of the major partner conflict areas.

Too many businesses have been ruined due to a

breakdown in communication between partners or the feeling of one taking advantage of the other's hard work. Planning and spending time to set the parameters of the relationship will reduce the possibility of a company-ending dispute.

Lesson 3 Takeaways...

✓ There are both major benefits and drawbacks to having a business partner, and you need to consider them before acting.

✓ Set out expectations in writing, create clear lines of communication, and define the roles in the business.

✓ Plan in the event of a "business divorce" by agreeing to certain terms, like how to value or divide the business, to make it fair and clear from the beginning.

LESSON 4

CHOOSE THE RIGHT ENTITY FOR RUNNING YOUR BUSINESS

Understanding business entities and which one is right for your business is one of the most popular questions for anyone starting up, especially when you have a partner. With multiple options to choose from, and being unsure whether you even need to form one, we will explore how you can start to determine what is right for you.

You don't need to register a corporation to start a business. There is a misconception that you need a separate entity to start selling. If you stand on the corner, selling lemonade, you have started a business, albeit a very small one. You may need some licenses and permits to do this properly, as discussed earlier, but having a corporation does not legally change whether you can sell that lemonade.

At the beginning of your side hustle, you may not need to register an entity, but as you grow, take on additional financial obligations, and have more chances for something to go wrong, there are significant advantages to doing so. When talking about entity types, there are a few that most commonly come up. To understand the options, let's take a look at the various forms a business can take.

SOLE PROPRIETORSHIP

First, there is the sole proprietorship. A sole proprietorship is merely when someone conducts business, individually, with no legal distinction between the business and its owner. If you grab a wholesale box of candy bars and sell them at a baseball game, you are doing business as a sole proprietor. You pay taxes on your earning as an individual, and if someone gets sick from your candy bars, they will be suing you personally for the damages they incur. As you can tell, this is the most basic form that a business can take.

GENERAL PARTNERSHIP

Next, there is the general partnership. Although partnerships have complex law behind them and are best when organized according to a written partnership agreement, they are extremely simple to create. The law states that whenever two or more persons do business together in pursuit of a profit, they are engaged in a general partnership.

If you decide to start selling more products at

those baseball games, and you want to do it with your friend that has great experience in selling not only candy bars but also hotdogs, you might be forming a general partnership without even realizing it. Without proper planning and understanding between you and your buddy, it could lead to a nasty fight if one of you thinks you deserve more than you're getting or if you didn't realize you started a legal partnership.

General partnerships are easy to form, since they are the default state when more than one person is owning a business, but they offer no protection for the owners. General partnerships are defined by their "pass through" liability and taxation. That is, general partnerships are businesses, but they don't set up any legal barriers between you, your partners, and the business. If something goes wrong and a lawsuit is filed, your personal assets will be on the hook, just like with the sole proprietorship. However, in a partnership, you also share liability for the acts of your other partners. If your partner injured someone while making a delivery, you will get dragged into the lawsuit and threatened that you and your personal assets are equally at risk for paying the damages.

Additionally, the partners in a general partnership will be taxed as individuals on whatever they earn. In many instances, this can be better for a small business, as it avoids "double taxation," where a business is taxed on profits at the company level and the owners are also taxed on the income they take from the business. With flow through taxation, the profits and losses are reflected on the owners' individual tax returns, so tax isn't due "twice."

There are other types of partnerships beyond the

general partnership, but they involve registration and are applicable to special circumstances. Limited partnerships ("LP") are a type of partnership that allow some of the partners to be under "limited" status. This allows them to invest in the partnership and share in the profits, but they do not have any input in the management of the business. In exchange, limited partners are able to shield themselves from some liability for claims against the business. There are also limited liability partnerships ("LLP"). These are reserved for licensed professionals like accountants and lawyers. They give the flexibility of a partnership and pass through taxation but grant liability protection like a corporation. However, since they are only allowed for certain licensed professionals, they aren't an option for most side hustles.

CORPORATION

Although the sole proprietorship and partnership are the easiest business types to create, one of the most ubiquitous is the corporation.

Corporations are separate legal entities from their owners. They can bring lawsuits and they can be sued like an individual. This is where the infamous "corporations are people" idea stems from. Unlike sole proprietorships and partnerships, corporations offer their owners limited liability protection. This means that if people acting on behalf of the corporation do something wrong, it is going to be an uphill battle for someone to sue the corporation's owners personally. The corporate form offers a layer of protection between the business and the owners that can be extremely valuable.

There are multiple types of corporations. In addition to general stock corporations, there are non-profits, social purpose and benefit corporations, professional corporations, and close corporations. Non-profits come in several flavors themselves, but the primary distinction is that non-profits do not have shareholders and thus cannot distribute any excess money they generate. The profits must be spent in pursuit of its charitable purpose on behalf of members or the public. Social purpose corporations and benefit corporations (often called B-Corps) are hybrid entities that can pursue profits but also have legal obligations to support a social or environmental mission decided by the corporation. Additionally, close corporations are for-profit corporations that must stay under a maximum number of owners but then allow the owners to operate without following many of the standard formalities, like annual meetings and documentation rules. Even with close corporations, the corporate form is more strictly defined than alternatives like the LLC, and there is a longer history of court decisions involving corporate law, which can possibly lead to more predictability in certain disputes.

Corporations also have a variety of tax types. For small business with limited owners, a corporation can file an "S" election with the IRS to avoid double taxation. The "S" refers to Subchapter "S" of Title 26 of the United States Code, and corporations that make this filing are commonly called S-Corps in contrast to the default C-Corp under Subchapter "C."

Without an "S" election, a corporation must pay its own income tax in addition to the income tax its owners will pay when they receive funds. When you are a small business, you will typically want to reduce formalities and corporate income tax until having those would actually be beneficial.

While a corporation grants limited liability to its owners, it is important to note that this does not mean zero liability. There are certain situations that can either cause a court to disregard the limited liability status or where the status will not apply to protect the owners. Situations where the owners treat the corporation as only a shell, where they don't keep sufficient money in the corporation to pay its bills, and where they ignore the rules about how they hold meetings or vote in officers and director can lead to this. Additionally, acts by the owners that lead to certain catastrophic injuries or fraud can fall outside the limited liability cover. Despite this, there are steps you can take internally to run a corporation such that you can take advantage of the special protection.

LIMITED LIABILITY COMPANY

Another way to achieve limited liability is with the limited liability company ("LLC"). The LLC is the most popular structure for businesses in the United States. LLCs are generally less strict in their procedures when compared with typical corporations. These companies combine the limited liability protection of a corporation with the default pass through taxation status of a partnership. Additionally, they offer significant flexibility when it comes to structure and formalities. For example, where a typical corporation might require yearly annual meetings of the shareholders and the board of directors with the preparation of written minutes, an LLC doesn't require these by default. LLCs are either run directly by their members (the owners) or by a designated manager or a team of managers; there is no need to deal with the shareholder, director, and officer distinctions that exist in corporations.

For many small businesses and side hustles, an LLC is a simple route to choose, but it isn't perfect for every instance. Both corporations and LLCs must pay a franchise tax fee to operate in California of about $800 per year; however, LLCs also must pay tax on its gross receipt of funds once the business is generating revenue of over $250,000 per year. Your side hustle will be some ways off from making that much when you start, yet it is still something to consider.

LLCs can use the default method of counting ownership in the terms of membership percentages, or you can write the organizational documents to allow for ownership in stock-like interests similar to corporations. That is, you can hold percentage of ownership, like a partnership where two owners might split it 50% to each, or it can give its owners "units" so that the two owners might each hold 5,000 units to reflect this. It all depends on how you set it up.

LLCs are also popular for passive income businesses like real estate holdings. By using an LLC, as opposed to holding an investment property in your own name, you can limit the potential exposure to your personal wealth. At the same time, you aren't as restricted in structure and formalities as you would be with a corporation. Since these types of passive income businesses don't intend on growing and scaling by adding shareholders and employees as the enterprise expands, the simple but flexible form of LLC is enough for many situations. You can always convert your business into a different form later—you'll just have to pay to handle all the paperwork.

FORMING IN ANOTHER STATE

With a general understanding of the primary business forms, the next question people typically ask is: "What about Delaware?"

Many business owners are interested in forming their business in a state outside of the one they intend to operate in. There are a few reasons for looking at forming your company in another state, but many of these will not provide significant benefits to a side hustle or new small business, especially when compared with the administrative costs and hassles of doing so.

A primary reason people look to alternative states for registration is taxation. Some states, like Nevada, have favorable tax climates. Nevada does not charge corporate income tax, does not tax shares, and does not charge an annual franchise tax. It sounds great, but this isn't the whole picture. When you register in another state, you must still register as "foreign" company in the state you physically operate in. This will subject you to that state's tax laws too. The benefits you obtain from forming in another state will not prevent the state where you operate in from taxing you. This is a common misconception about the benefits from foreign registration and is largely beneficial only if you plan on operating in multiple states.

Another reason for foreign registration is taking advantage of a "business-friendly" legal climate. Some states have laws more favorable to the board of directors, which is attractive for larger, publicly listed companies. Some states, like Delaware, have special courts set up to handle business cases and can be quicker and more familiar in resolving their corporate disputes.

The downside to registering in a foreign state is dealing with multiple states for compliance. By registering in Wyoming, but operating primarily in Ohio, for example, you need to maintain your entity and remain in good standing in both states. It also exposes you to potentially being sued in Wyoming, which could prove inconvenient.

Ultimately, if you choose to register a corporation or LLC out of state, it is going to depend on your individual situation and whether the benefits of foreign registration are worth the potential extra costs and administrative work.

FICTITIOUS BUSINESS NAMES

Regardless of the form your business takes, there is always the important question of what your business is named. If you register a corporation or LLC, you'll be required to give it a business name. There are specific words that need to be applied to the name to allow it to be registered. For a corporation, you typically need the name to end with Corporation, Corp., Inc., Limited, or similar indicator. The historical reason for this was to signal to the public that the business had limited liability status and that recourse to the owners was not the same as non-incorporated companies. While this does not have as much practical use today, the naming conventions are still generally required when you go to register.

Beyond legally naming your business when you register an entity, you have the ability to apply a legal name to any business. This is called a fictitious business name. Businesses that are either not registered or that want to operate under a separate name will generally apply for one in the county in which they are located and operating. This allows the business to operate with a name different from the owner's name.

Let's say Sara and Kurt form a corporation called Cutesy Creatures, Inc. If they start another venture under that company, they might apply for a fictitious business name to publicly do business under a different moniker. Maybe they want to start selling a set of horror-themed dolls as a part of the business, but they do not want it outwardly associated with Cutesy Creatures. The horror dolls and the cute plush toys are clearly different brands targeting different consumers. However, Sara and Kurt internally consider this part of the same company and do not want to split up the processes or finances. They also don't want to deal with forming another entity and paying another franchise tax or registration fee. By using a fictitious business name, Sara and Kurt could achieve an outward separation while keeping it one company on the inside. They could sign contracts, open a bank account, or do other actions through "Cutesy Creatures, Inc. d.b.a. Zombie Dolls Company" and use the name "Zombie Dolls Company" as their own.

Fictitious business names are also useful for sole proprietorships. If you don't register an entity, a fictitious business name gives you the ability to operate the business more formally and separate from your own name alone.

A fictitious business name does not legally do anything to the structure of your business. It does not create any liability protection or change your taxes. In essence, it is just a nickname. A fictitious business name also is very easy to obtain, and it involves only filing simple forms and nominal registration fees to obtain. For many side hustlers, operating with a fictitious business name is going to be sufficient until the business gets big enough for the cost of creating a formal structure to make more sense.

TAXPAYER IDENTIFICATION NUMBERS

If the articles of incorporation is the birth certificate for your company, then the taxpayer identification number ("TIN") is the social security number. This number, also referred to as an employer identification number or EIN, is the number used by the IRS for tracking business income and related information. You can apply for a TIN, even if you do not choose a corporation, LLC, or other registered entity to run your business. You can operate a sole proprietorship out of the trunk of your car and still apply for a TIN.

The primary reasons you would need a TIN in a non-registered entity is if you are going to hire an employee or create a retirement plan. You may also need one to apply for certain licenses and permits. You will need one regardless of whether you register an entity. Luckily, this process is straightforward, quick, and free. The IRS wants to make it easy to collect taxes from you.

CHARACTER EXAMPLE

Luis is in the food space. The food industry is filled with potential liabilities. Contamination and customers becoming ill from your product are major concerns. This is partially why there are so many health and safety regulations for food preparation and storage. If someone gets sick, Luis might need to issue a recall or he could get sued for the damages caused. All this for some taffy? Hopefully no, but it is possible.

Consider also Luis' personal circumstances and the present size of his business. Luis is a college student and he has sizable student loan debt and isn't from a notably wealthy family. When there is a potential civil lawsuit, the plaintiff would be considering whether they will even be able to recover the money they could win from the case. Without assets to protect by putting up a limited liability shield, does Luis need to go through the time and expense of creating a corporation or LLC?

Luis' business is only doing a couple thousand dollars in revenue per year and he is not expecting it to grow at this time since he is not aggressively pursuing sales. There is real potential to grow, but at this point, Luis is not putting much in his pocket after paying the costs and expenses associated with his side hustle. If he formed a corporation, the yearly franchise tax fee might be too heavy of an expense for him to carry at this stage.

For the time being, Luis might consider keeping with his sole proprietorship and applying for a fictitious business name. He can create a business bank account owned by "Luis L'Astname d.b.a. Little L. Taffy" and start operating as Little L. Taffy.

Now, let's consider Sara. She has started her business, but she is looking to her friend Kurt to help out. They agreed to become partners with Sara owning 60% of the business and Kurt owning 40%. They will still need to consider what business form to use.

As a default, Sara and Kurt would become a general partnership. The basic act of going into business together could turn Sara's sole proprietorship into a partnership. Even if they want to stick with a general partnership, Sara and Kurt will want to write out the terms of their deal and execute a written partnership agreement. This would include basic terms about what they contributed, how decisions are made, and what will happen if they don't want to stay in business together in the future. Before concluding on the form, Sara should consider some other factors as well.

As far as potential injury goes, Sara's business may have lower risk than Luis', assuming she sources her product parts from a reputable manufacturer. But

Sara must further consider their financial positions. Sara has a stable career and has contributed to her retirement and savings accounts. Kurt's other projects, as a consultant and web designer, should be considered too. They might be interested in keeping their personal assets and company liability separated, since they both have more to lose. Sara and Kurt would value the peace of mind from separating personal and business assets and liabilities officially.

With an LLC, she could issue ownership to Kurt by giving him membership interest. In doing so, Sara could write out a contract where Kurt agrees to specified, reasonable performance requirements to obtain his ownership over time. For example, they could agree that Kurt gets a 40% interest immediately, but if he stops working in the business within certain period in the future, he would lose out on part of his interest. For example, if he left working for the company after one year into the business, he would only be entitled to keep 10%, but for each subsequent year he remains active, he is entitled to keep 10% more interest until he reaches the full 40% without any restrictions. This is referred to as a vesting schedule, and it would allow Sara some assurance that Kurt would continue to perform his duties for the company, rather than risking him obtaining his 40% immediately and then slacking off or having a personal crisis that prevents him from getting his work done.

If Sara and Kurt were co-founding the business together initially, then they might consider the corporate structure with option agreement for each of them. They could start off obtaining 1,000 shares each to become 50/50 partners. Then, for the next five years, they have the option to purchase 1,000 more shares at the end of each year at the same initial value so long they are active in the business and are meeting their defined goals and contributions. Under this approach, if one of them stops committing their hard work into the company, but doesn't want to give up their ownership, the other can slowly acquire a larger interest and not feel as betrayed. There are tax implications to any approach that will need to be considered too.

Although people may have the best intentions today, there's no telling what will happen in the future. An LLC or corporation would give Sara and Kurt the limited liability protection they want and help to separate the financials of the business from themselves as individuals. They can combine this approach with an employment contract to bolster their assurances to each other.

Turning our attention again, we can address Myra. Myra is our only business owner that has potential interest from an investor that has no interest in actively working for the business. Given that she is looking at possible outside investment from her uncle, she might consider using a corporation.

There is no hard and fast rule, but many investors prefer a business that is structured as a corporation. One reason is the default structure and formalities for a corporation. The owners (the shareholders) elect a board of directors, who then, in turn, elect corporate officers (president, chief financial officer, secretary) to carry out the business of the corporation. Investors may prefer this structure because it allows them to negotiate a seat on the board of directors to encourage accountability and gain some control. Corporations have default rules about meetings and reporting information to the owners that can be attractive. Institutional investors also sometimes prefer default tax status corporations ("C-Corps") and keep a portfolio of business investments with only that type for tax reasons.

With all this said, investors regularly put money into all sorts of business types. Myra, and you, must consider all the facts to determine which entity will work best for your situation and then work with an attorney and accountant to set it up properly.

Lesson 4 Takeaways...

✓ If you start a business alone, it's a sole proprietorship by default.

✓ If you work on a business with a co-owner, it's a general partnership by default. A written agreement should be prepared, but it is not technically required.

✓ Corporations and limited liability companies are registered entities that provide liability protection for the owners as well as certain tax advantages, but you may owe a yearly minimum franchise tax or other fee, depending on the states in which you operate.

✓ You can obtain a fictitious business name or taxpayer identification number for any type of business.

LESSON 5

CONSIDER BUYING INSURANCE

Regardless of how you choose to structure your business, insurance is an important and often forgotten form of protection for new business. It may not seem as interesting as forming a corporation, but it can be just as important.

No one wants to pay for insurance. It can feel like throwing money away on something you don't use. This is especially so for the types of insurance that you would get for your business. Unlike having health insurance, for example, which provides you with pre-negotiated rates for the costs of a doctor's visit, the business insurance policies are best if you never have to use them at all. So why pay money for something you hope to never need? One word: Risk. If your business is the boat, then insurance is the life jacket. You will be drowning if you have no coverage when something goes wrong. Although we like to avoid walking under open ladders and try to keep a four-leaf clover on our lapels, the reality is that accidents and mistakes do happen.

Of course, insurance does cost money. You're paying now for the hope that nothing happens and that you never need to use it. When we put it like that, it can sound unappetizing, but it is a way to reduce risk. It doesn't guarantee that your business survives, but it makes the bad times less bad. It allows you to face the future with more certainty by knowing you've got a crutch to lean on and that a surprise volcano will not burn down your hard work entirely.

Specifically, an insurance policy will pay for the damages that are within the scope of the coverage. The policy will also pay for hiring a lawyer to defend you if a lawsuit is filed. The policy provides a pool of money that will get used to resolve the matter, so the amount of coverage on the policy is important.

Here is a brief overview of the types of insurance to consider obtaining to help protect your business.

General Liability Insurance

As the name suggests, general liability insurance is general. In essence, general liability insurance helps when a third party (someone not part of your business) sues your company for property damage, bodily injury, or advertising and personal damages. This would include an instance where someone claims that your business caused a physical harm to someone. It might also cover where there is damage to rented property you are using for your business. It could also include an instance where someone claims you slandered them and harmed their reputation.

When your business gets to a certain level, you

would benefit from general liability coverage. There are an untold number of situations where customers, competitors, employees, or vendors might make a claim against you. Once you get to the point where a lawsuit like this could destroy your business, insurance could help pay for lawyers to defend you or put money toward settling the claim.

Professional Liability Insurance

Professional liability insurance is also referred to as errors and omissions insurance or malpractice insurance. This type of insurance specifically covers claims against your business that arise from a professional service that you are providing. If a third party sues your business for providing incomplete or defective work or for an error you made, then professional liability insurance can kick in.

Service providers should especially look into this. If you are doing handy work and you accidentally cause damage while trying to fix something, it can help. If you are an outside bookkeeper and you make a mistake causing your client harm, it can help. These types of claims can be some of the most expensive harms that you could get sued over because the claims include the losses that your client has faced due to your error, which can be huge.

Business Property Insurance

Business property insurance can protect both the physical location of a business as well as things like tools, equipment, and inventory. Anyone that is worried about risks to the physical property of their business should look into it. For example, someone like Sara, who might one day have thousands of dollars of her plush creature inventory stored at any time, could get a policy to protect her in the event the facility floods and ruins all her extra inventory and label printers.

Worker's Compensation Insurance

Worker's compensation insurance covers medical payments and portions of lost wages for workers that are injured while on the job. It can also help pay for employee rehabilitation and wrongful death benefits in case there is a serious accident. If you hire an employee, you will need worker's compensation insurance. If someone is operating a sole proprietorship and is the only person in their business, they can still purchase worker's compensation insurance to cover themselves.

In many states, worker's compensation is a special system that completely replaces the right for a worker to sue their employer for work-related injuries. When you think of worker's compensation, you likely are thinking of accidents like crashing a forklift or falling off a ladder, but there are many types of claims that could be made against you that worker's compensation can cover. This would even include repetitive stress injuries that can occur in office jobs, such as carpal tunnel syndrome or tendonitis.

Product Liability Insurance

Product liability insurance protects your business from claims made for damage caused by the products you have sold or supplied. If you're selling a product with the possibility of causing harm or having a defect, you should consider product liability insurance once you start selling enough to justify that expense. This is especially true if you're selling anything with a higher chance of something going wrong. If you are selling a product with electronic components, what if it explodes in someone's hands and permanently scars them? Having an insurance policy could prevent one small mistake from potentially ruining your business.

Commercial Vehicle Insurance

Commercial vehicle insurance covers physical and property damage related to automobile usage that falls outside a personal vehicle insurance policy. You are already going to be required to carry personal insurance if you have a car, but your business may require use of your car or obtaining its own company van. If your business is dependent on your vehicle, such as for making deliveries or getting to a gig location, imagine having an accident on your way. If you're carrying expensive equipment or inventory, you want to make sure you're protected because your standard auto policy may not cut it. If you do not have a current vehicle insurance policy that will cover your business activity, then it could be a reason for the insurance company to deny covering your accident claim, so check your existing car insurance either way.

CHARACTER EXAMPLE

Let's look at Alex, who is a good candidate for insurance. He is holding dance classes, and anything involving physical activity increases the risks for injury. Whether it's someone tripping while doing a reverse turn or breaking a hip while doing the moonwalk, the risk is real.

Since Alex is renting space from his friend's yoga studio, the first question he needs to ask is what insurance does the studio has and whether it will extend coverage for Alex's classes. This is something Alex can find out by talking to his friend and possibly the landlord for the building. Alex should ask about any policies in place or even take a look at the studio's lease to see what the insurance requirements there might be. Depending on the details of the lease, many commercial landlords will require minimum insurance coverage to be held by their tenants. Alex's classes could be covered already, so it is important to read any potentially applicable policy documents.

Either way, Alex might take out a general liability policy and ensure it covers his students. If there is an accident, the insurance can kick in to help with the medical bills. Alex's entire livelihood and future could be ruined from just one simple accident. We all hope these days never come, but it's worth being prepared if they do. At this time, Alex has no other employees, but he also could obtain worker's compensation insurance in the event Alex gets injured. Even a small policy can help protect the future.

Lesson 5 Takeaways...

✓ There are many types of insurance available to protect a business. As your company grows, you will need to add more layers of protection.

✓ If you never have to use your insurance, then you should consider it a good thing. You are paying for protection and mitigating risks.

✓ Your personal car insurance may not cover your business activities in the event of an accident, so call your insurance agent.

LESSON 6

UNDERSTAND THE BASICS OF INTELLECTUAL PROPERTY

Intellectual property is often misunderstood. At its core, intellectual property is the term we use to refer to the various rights associated with intangible property and ideas. We will introduce the basic terms used and types of intellectual property and then apply these to some examples.

Copyrights, trademarks, patents, and trade secrets. These are the four major types of intellectual property that are generally implied when that phrase is used. Intellectual property has different origins, yet they all share the common characteristic that they are intangible property. They are property, which exist separate from their physical form, as opposed real estate or tangible objects. Although some types of intellectual property might adopt a physical form, like a page of sheet music or a sculpture, the rights themselves control the ideas behind the objects. Intellectual property is an important concept in business, which can spell the difference between success and failure.

COPYRIGHT

Copyright is commonly mistaken with trademark, but they are entirely different concepts. In the United States, copyright is a form of intellectual property that originally comes from the U.S. Constitution. Article I, Section 8, Clause 8 states that Congress has the power "[t]o promote the progress of science and useful arts, by securing for limited times to authors and inventors the exclusive right to their respective writings and discoveries." Since then, Congress has passed more laws on the topic. The comprehensive Copyright Act of 1976 sets up a general framework, definitions, and processes related to copyrights in this country. There are many additional laws, regulations, and international treaties that affect copyrights worldwide.

In legal terms, copyrights are granted for original works of authorship that are fixed in a tangible medium of expression. In short, it protects a thing that you make up yourself, whether formally published or not, that is set in fixed manner. Copyrights are created the moment you "fix" that work.

Let's try a quick exercise to illustrate. First, take out a pen and paper. Second, scribble some random marks on that paper. Add another one. And there you go—you just created a copyrighted work! It's original and fixed in a tangible form. However, it isn't just items on a piece of paper. Examples of copyrightable works include websites, writings, drawings, designs, photos, videos, recorded or written music, sculptures, and compilations of information. Derivative works are also subject to copyright, such as drawing a similar-looking character like Mickey "Moose" or making the sequel to a movie.

While a copyright is created once the work is fixed, you can register your copyright with the United States Copyright Office for extra protection through a relatively simple process. If you believe that someone might try to steal your work, it can be a good idea to register and gain some additional legal protection.

CHARACTER EXAMPLE

Sara has illustrated and written some children's books that feature her cast of characters. While writing, Sara is securing copyright protection in the written words. She doesn't have to actually publish or register anything to get those rights as long as the work itself is original and meets the other requirements to secure protection. Sara can take more steps to secure the rights, such as placing a copyright notice (e.g., "2019 © Sara Surname"), but this isn't a hard rule. In general, if someone rips off the book's words and images, Sara can make a claim to shut that infringer down if she can prove she owns the rights.

There is also Myra, who has been creating recipes as part of her business to use in her app. Are these recipes subject to copyright protection? Unfortunately for her, no. The mere listing of ingredients can't be protected. Although many forms of art or writings are protectable, some are deemed outside the scope of copyright. Fashion designs, for instance, are not subject to copyright protection. This is why there are so many fashion knockoffs by major brands looking the same except for using an altered fabric pattern or having a prominent designer logo. Since the recipes themselves are not protectable, this means she can gather recipes from other sources and include them in her app. However, she will need to be careful not to directly take the written instructions themselves because that part of the recipe could constitute a written, copyrightable piece of text, even if the underlying recipe could be reproduced without issue.

TRADEMARK

A business' brand can be one of its most crucial aspects. This is where trademarks come in. Trademarks are the logos, names, or other distinguishing characteristics that help people determine the origin of some product or service. Unlike copyrights, which are protectable in and of themselves, trademarks are only protected when they are associated with some product or service.

Trademarks are intended to help people understand the source of something presented for sale in a market. If you are going to pay $400 for a brand name purse, then you would look to and rely on the luxury brand logo that the purse carries to justify the price. You might pay more for an Apple computer, even if functionally it is the same as a lower-priced competitor. In the abstract, the marks are not protected because the protection is tied to offering something in commerce. Yet, marks can also be subject to copyright protection. For example, Disney has claimed copyright protection over various

Mickey Mouse cartoons, but the company has also claimed trademark protection because Mickey's name and face are so iconic and associated with that company.

Contrary to popular belief, you don't need to register a trademark to have a trademark. As you continue to use a distinguishing mark as part of your business, you begin to build up your rights in that mark. These are called "common law" trademark rights and exist in connection with the state you are operating in.

However, many choose to register and obtain the legal benefits. Trademarks are registered through the United States Patent and Trademark Office for federal protection. Federal registration is not prohibitively expensive and grants significant upside, such as gaining legal presumptive ownership, using the registration to stop imports of counterfeiting products, accessing statutory damages if you file a lawsuit against an infringer, and more. As an alternative to federal registration, state governments also allow registration for marks that are used in their state. It is a somewhat less difficult process to obtain state registration, but it does not have the full slew of benefits that federal registration does.

Another aspect of trademark law is the concept of trade dress. This is a form of intellectual property that relates to the promotion of a product or service, and it usually takes the form of packaging and decor. Trade dress covers the total image and presentation of a product, which can include size, shape, color, texture, and more. To get trade dress protection, there must be some "secondary meaning" associated with it. That is, the size and other attributes make consumers think of a particular source.

For example, while Starbucks Coffee can claim a trademark in the name Starbucks, the mermaid logo, and other aspects of the business, it cannot necessarily claim a trademark in their use of green aprons, the unique look of their menu boards, or the font used on the food case—the aspects that signal to you: "Hey, I'm in a Starbucks." If someone opened a competing coffee shop looking identical to a Starbucks but called themselves Henry's Coffee, Starbucks may still have a claim for trade dress infringement.

In fact, this sort of happened in 2014, when comedian Nathan Fielder opened a short-lived store in Los Angeles. The parody store, carrying the name "Dumb Starbucks," was set up to look exactly like a Starbucks Coffee location, except that everything on the menu was "dumb." There was a dumb latte, a dumb macchiato—you get the idea. Beyond the fact that the uses of the Starbucks name and logo were clear trademark infringement, the method of copying the look and layout of a real store gave rise to trade dress issues. This whole experiment ended when the local health department shut down the store before Starbucks took any legal action themselves, but it served as a funny example of these concepts in practice.

Trademarks are incredibly important for a business of any size because it is in part what makes your business more than a generic commodity. Your brand captures and stores the goodwill for your business that is generated as you make your customers and clients happy. Brand and brand identity can be some of the most valuable parts of a business. Given not only the marketing expenses to promote a brand but also the benefits that exist from having done so, it is vital that you take steps to protect you company's identity.

CHARACTER EXAMPLE

Sara has worked hard coming up with her business name and logo. With her background in illustration, she was able to come up with a unique way of presenting the name of her company in a cute, curly font, as well as creating a koala bear drawing as the logo. She has been using these marks for some time and receives positive feedback from customers. As a result, Sara is looking at trademarks as the way to protect her branding.

Sara has some choices. Sara can continue using her business name and logo with her product by putting it on her website, the tags for the products, and business cards. This is the first step. By using the marks, she acquires "common law" trademark rights. If someone starts using a confusingly similar name or logo with the same types of goods as she offers, she could issue a cease and desist demand or challenge it in court. However, since the mark is not registered, she would have to prove her ownership of the marks and also prove exactly how she was damaged, which can involve expensive analysis and lengthy litigation. For example, she might think she lost some sales when a competing business calling itself "Cutesy Monsters" appeared online and used an almost identical font and logo, except that the monster logo had three eyes instead of the two eyes on Sara's koala.

Part of the benefits of a registered trademark is the availability of enhanced damages in a federal case and the ability to seek her attorney fees against an infringer. She would also be permitted to use the registration symbol (®) with her registered marks.

Sara wants to register her marks, but she isn't sure exactly what to do. For starters, a trademark has to be tied with a certain good or service available in commerce. Since Sara is selling her plushies under the name Cutesy Creatures with her koala logo, she has this box checked. Next, we have to consider the marks. Trademarks exist in a number of forms. Here, there are at least three. First, there is the name without any stylizing or art as the name in plain text itself. Next, there is the stylized wording. This is the artistic presentation of the name and the way the words are laid out. If Sara wants to keep someone from using a different name but with the very similar stylized words, then she might want to register both. Third, she has her koala logo. She can register the koala bear logo separately from the words if she desires.

It is key that Sara—and you—think through the key parts of your branding and prepare a plan for protecting this investment as the business grows.

PATENT AND TRADE SECRETS

The other two major forms of intellectual property that we will cover are patents and trade secrets. We will briefly address these to help distinguish them from trademarks and copyright.

A patent is the right to an invention that is granted to its inventor. A United States patent allows you to prevent other people from making, using, or selling your invention in the country and also prevents someone from importing a copy of your invention from another country. When you apply for patent protection through the federal government, the materials explaining your invention and how it works will be publicly available. This is out of necessity because other people need to have access to the information on what they are being excluded from doing themselves. However, this means that your formula or design could be knocked off and altered to try and "get around" your patent by others, even if you have the legal right to stop them from doing it.

For those that fear their proprietary information being exposed to the public, this is where trade secrets come in. Trade secrets are proprietary devices, techniques, processes, or information that are confidentially maintained by a company. Trade secrets might include client lists, special methods for manufacturing products, or even secret recipes, like the formula to Coca-Cola or KFC. Unlike other forms of intellectual property, trade secrets can't be registered because the act of keeping them secret and away from the public is a necessary part of their existence. The value of a trade secret comes from the economic advantage that it provides to the business that keeps it secure.

CHARACTER EXAMPLE

Let's say Luis has come up with a more efficient way of making his taffy. He also developed a new type of wrapper to keep his taffy fresher for longer than the traditional wax paper used by other candy companies.

Luis has some choices to make if he wants to keep his intellectual property secure.

For his new production method, Luis could find a lawyer and try to register a patent. However, he will have to disclose the new method as part of the patent application process. Even if it gets granted and he has the right to stop someone else from using his special process, how will he know if someone is ripping him off in their own kitchen? Maybe in this instance, trade secret protection would be appropriate. Luis can write out the method and keep it in a secure file marked "confidential." He could keep his process secret from others, except people that he might be working with. If he has to disclose the method to someone like a vendor or future employee, he could ask that they sign a basic non-disclosure agreement to keep the information private.

Turning to Luis' new wrapper, the circumstances might be different. The wrapper looks like wax paper, but it works better. Since the wrapper is already out in public, he wouldn't be risking much by attempting to seek patent protection. He also would know if other businesses are infringing by making knock off wrappers, since he might see them in shops or advertised online. With a patent, he could potentially license the right to use the material to a big company and enjoy a mostly passive income stream.

AVOID STEALING INTELLECTUAL PROPERTY

For works subject to intellectual property protections, you will need to be mindful of other people's rights and avoid violating them. It is just as important that you protect your own property as you avoid trampling the rights of others. If you end up infringing, there can be serious consequences.

As discussed at the beginning of this book, the internet has made it easy and accessible to start a business. With all the availability of information, there is also a massive availability and ease of using content created by others, without permission. There are a number of international treaties that have attempted to address this. For example, the Digital Millennium Copyright Act is a federal law that implemented two treaties from the World Intellectual Property Organization. You may be familiar with this law, as platforms like YouTube cite it when they receive "takedown" requests from copyright holders for illegally hosted content. Since filing lawsuits against everyone that infringes on copyright is infeasible, this is a swift and simple means for people and organizations trying to protect their content.

It is incredibly easy to steal digital content, even by accident, but ignorance is not a defense. Although more casual forms of infringement are either ignored or simply removed, when there is a business accused of stealing content, the chances of being taken to court increase. Even a small e-commerce shop can be taken to court for tens of thousands of dollars for unknowingly importing and listing counterfeit products on a single occasion.

At the same time, not all intangible creations out there belong to a particular owner. Many of them are part of the public domain. Public domain means that the work, symbol, or other content is not being protected through some manner of intellectual property. To help understand the relationship, some have described work belonging to the public domain as the general rule, while intellectual property protection as the exception. But unless you are certain a work is public domain, it is critical that you respect the rights of others.

FAIR USE

With the two camps shown—protected material and public domain material—you might be thinking: What about fair use? In copyright law, fair use is the doctrine that attempts to balance the right of a copyright holder to restrict the use of their protected works against the right of the people to free speech and expression. Needless to say, this is a complicated and ever-shifting balancing act.

The general rule of fair use is that limited portions of copyrighted material may be replicated or modified for purposes of criticism, teaching, and reporting without obtaining permission from the author. Section 107 of the Copyright Act provides several considerations to determine whether an unlicensed use of copyrighted material constitutes a valid exercise under fair use. These considerations are:

- Purpose and character of the use, including whether the use is of a commercial nature or is for non-profit educational purposes;
- Nature of the copyrighted work;
- Amount and substantiality of the portion used in relation to the copyrighted work as a whole; and
- Effect of the use upon the potential market or value of the copyrighted work.

An interesting case involving fair use law came about in 2016 in *Hosseinzadeh v. Klein*. In that case, a popular YouTube channel was accused of copyright infringement and defamation by another channel. The video in question featured the creators, Ethan and Hila Klein, making a reaction-style parody video of a comedic pick-up-artist type video. The plaintiff, who had created it, argued that use of clips from his own video created grounds for the suit and that the negative comments harmed his reputation. To many people's delight, the court disagreed with the plaintiff and dismissed the case, finding that the Kleins were engaged in "critical commentary" that was not actionable. Even though the Kleins were successful, they incurred substantial attorney fees to defend themselves. The fact is that seemingly innocent online acts can have real world consequences.

One area where fair use does not apply is purely commercial reproductions. This is seen constantly on marketplace sites. If you search any popular characters or brands on online markets or t-shirt printing sites, you are bound to find hundreds of goods for sale. Most, and likely all, of those goods are violating the intellectual property rights protecting those characters. These sites will follow takedown demands by the rights holders, but usually these shops are too small and too numerous for large companies to stomp them out entirely. While many people get away with infringing on this content, they are on the wrong side of the law. If your goal is to build a sustainable and legitimate business, you'll want to avoid this false shortcut.

LICENSING MATERIALS

The best way to go about using material protected by intellectual property that you did not create is to obtain a license. Material under a Creative Commons license has been designated by the author as freely useable, usually under only very limited restrictions such as requiring attribution. Alternatively, there are many stock image and sound companies that will provide licenses to use their content libraries for a fee, including for most commercial use. As a business, it is key you read any license you are obtaining to use someone else's content to ensure your planned uses fall within the scope that is granted to you.

Recently, there has been extraordinary popularity in video game streaming through online platforms like YouTube and Twitch. Normally, one might be walking into copyright infringement by recording footage of a video game and uploading it online. Yet, many publishers have found a major advantage in allowing their games to be played, recorded, and shared online, which both acts as free advertising and also supports the creation of a more engaged and resilient fan base. If you plan on recording a game or other footage, check the publisher's website for the terms and conditions they have for using their game material in your videos. For example, game publisher Square Enix, based in Japan, provides a number of conditions to allow footage of its games, including restricting the use for a commercial purpose, requiring a copyright notice attributing the company, and not allowing its use alongside offensive materials.

It is easy to steal content online, and you may have done it without even realizing. When you start using the internet to do business, you become more accountable and increase your chance of being noticed.

CHARACTER EXAMPLE

What if Myra wants to include a clip from her favorite song in one of her videos? If she uses it without permission, that could be copyright infringement. Myra's videos are for a business purpose, and the use of the song would be to introduce a special segment of the video. She is playing an unaltered clip of the music for ten seconds. As a result, she might get hit with a takedown notice or worse.

For many artists on major record labels, a license to use a song can be purchased through organizations like ASCAP, BMI, or similar rights holders. For less popular musicians, you can send a message to the band or the record label to ask permission directly and potentially negotiate a license. They might even be happy to lend their music if you give them a credit to help boost their own awareness and engage in cross-promotion.

Lesson 6 Takeaways...

✓ Copyrights protect fixed works, like pictures, songs, or writings.

✓ Trademarks protect the names, logos, or tag lines that distinguish your business from another.

✓ Patents protect processes and designs. Trade secrets are confidential information maintained by your business.

✓ Don't build your business by stealing other people's content. If you license material to use in your business, read the license and ensure it permits your planned uses.

LESSON 7

WATCH WHAT YOU SAY, EVEN ONLINE

Some people forget that what happens on the internet matters in the real world. Whether it's posting comments, listing on eBay, or saying something in a video, people are responsible for their actions online. There are practical realities with enforcing laws on the internet, which largely arise from expense, anonymity, and geography. But where money is involved, there is more incentive for companies and individuals to follow through. As your business grows, you become a worthier pursuit. Unlike an anonymous individual who might escape to the shadows, you have to keep your business out there in the marketplace to stay alive.

MISLEADING STATEMENTS AND ADVERTISING

While the internet still feels like the Wild West in many ways, there are numerous laws affecting what you do online. When businesses first began setting up virtual shops years ago, there was a lack of regulation and process to address legal issues. As time has passed, this has changed.

The Federal Trade Commission ("FTC") is the branch of the United States government charged with carrying out consumer protection. The FTC investigates and fines businesses that engage in unfair and deceptive practices and marketing. The FTC also has specific authority to address business activities online. Under the law, a practice is deceptive if a reasonable consumer is likely to be misled by a material statement or omission by a business. This includes where the statement or omission is likely to affect consumer choices. It is both the content and presentation of an advertisement or statement that are relevant. Although online formats are constantly evolving, the foundational principles of truth in advertising stay the same.

One aspect of this comes about in the FTC's guidelines on native advertising. The concept of native advertising involves paid media, such as articles, news stories, and other entertainment, that appears to follow the same form as a media outlet's non-advertising content. This often takes the shape of sponsored videos or posts.

Although you might never guess it if you checked your spam folder, another regulated area is email and other communications. The aptly named CAN-SPAM

Act regulates all commercial messages, which are defined as "any electronic mail message the primary purpose of which is the commercial advertisement or promotion of a commercial product or service." If you intend on sending business emails, such as to a mailing list that you have developed, you will need to comply with the law.

Under the CAN-SPAM Act, you will want to ensure that your commercial communications, at a minimum:

- Do not contain misleading or false header information or subject lines;
- Disclose that the communication is an advertisement in some manner;
- Provide a valid address; and
- Provide an opt-out process that you then follow.

There are many other laws and regulations related to claims you make enforced by both the FTC and private citizens, so you will want to be generally aware of the limits of what you can state about your business and how you make those statements, including online. If you end up marketing online to any part of Europe, you need to wrangle with the General Data Protection Regulation ("GDPR"), which has strict additional rules.

CHARACTER EXAMPLE

What if Luis starts listing "all natural and organic" on his taffy packaging and the description he uses online to promote it? Everyone everywhere seems to claim their food products or cosmetics are "all natural," and it is true there is no specific, single definition for this phrase. This is in contrast to the word "organic," which in most instances requires certification from the United States Department of Agriculture or other granting institution. If Luis' taffy has largely synthetic ingredients, and he has not obtained an organic certification, he cannot make a claim of "all natural" or "organic" about his product. That would clearly be false. Luis would be engaging in unfair and deceptive practices by doing so.

While it's unlikely that Luis' small operation will get on the FTC's radar, an angry consumer complaint could change that. The FTC has prosecuted a number of claims against businesses asserting "all natural" or similar advertisement on their products. For example, in 2016, the FTC went after a fairly small sun care company for using the phrase "100% natural" in its sunscreen description when the product, in fact, contained synthetic ingredients of dimethicone and caprylyl glycol. There is no doubt the company, like so many others, thought "Who cares?" when they disregarded the falsity of their statements.

There is no telling when a governmental agency will decide to pursue a claim against you. These seemingly small decisions, like the words used on packaging, can have detrimental consequences for your business that can be averted with planning and attention.

DEFAMATION

In business, your reputation is vital. A bad reputation can impact your existing customer base and keep future customers away. No one wants to buy from the pizza parlor that regularly messes up orders, stiffs its employees, or has cleanliness problems. Protecting your reputation is important, especially online, where the ready flow of information and review sites provide ample opportunity for disgruntled customers, upset workers, or scheming competitors to harm you.

Defamation occurs when someone makes a false statement that harms another's reputation. While there are exceptions and special circumstances, defamation comes in two forms: slander, which is spoken, and libel, which is written. These problems often come up in vlogs, review sites, articles, and social media.

One of the hardest parts of proving defamation in court is the element of falsity. Truth is an absolute defense to a claim for defamation, so if the statement falls in a grey area of mixing fact and fiction, then it's a rough war to wage. Opinions are even stickier. If the opinion implies facts, then you may have a claim for defamation, but a straight opinion is defensible.

It may not be worthwhile to file a lawsuit just because user CoolMike2234 lied about your business on a review site. But what about the platform he posted it on? Under Section 230 of the Federal Communications Decency Act, sites that allow user content are generally safe from lawsuits for defamatory statements made by their users. This immunity is not unlimited, but it creates a strong defense. At the same time, there are typically non-court means to at least get the content pulled through reporting violations of the site's terms and conditions.

CHARACTER EXAMPLE

Suppose Myra receives a barrage of negative comments on her videos and in the reviews of her mobile app. After investigating, Myra believes they link back to a single competitor that is running their own recipe app. Myra's first instinct is to turn on her camera and record a video. She wants to call out the competitor for what they've done and make her own negative statements about their app. However, Myra has never used the competitor's app and had no real knowledge of whether it works or not. She also can't say for certain that it was the competitor leaving the nasty statement; she is mostly following a hunch.

Rather than risking a defamatory statement or getting embroiled in a harsh battle, Myra is better off keeping her cool. Even beyond straight defamation, there are claims that can be brought for wrongful interference with another's economic opportunities due to certain actions people take. In this instance, Myra might consider disabling the comments on her videos, reporting them to the site moderators, and if need be, releasing a public statement about the attacks and the truth about her products, rather than trying to drag someone into the muck.

TERMS OF SERVICE

Beyond the laws affecting you, there are rules applicable to the various websites and online services you use. When you utilize these forums or services to conduct business, their rules are as real and powerful as the law. The terms of service for online marketplaces like eBay, Etsy, and Amazon operate like the municipal ordinances covering the farmers' markets or commercial zoning restrictions that you would face if you opened up a physical store. The difference is that, rather than having a complicated but well-intentioned legal process or court system created through public means, the online marketplace rules are typically designed to facilitate a dispute as quickly as possible and to protect the host company's image and bottom line.

Terms of service are the rules that a website owner or software creator imposes over your use and interaction with them. They are the house rules for the party, so remember to take off your shoes and use coasters on the coffee table.

Terms of service are a type of contract, and contracts generally can be thought of as private laws. Contracts are agreements on how two or more persons or businesses will behave with each other. Before websites and online services had click boxes for their terms of service, the law addressed shrinkwrap licenses that were part of physical software purchases. Manufacturers would insert a notice in the box, stating that the consumer was agreeing to whatever terms the manufacturer included by opening the shrinkwrap packaging. Court cases challenged it, but subject to certain exceptions, this practice was generally upheld.

Online and digitally, the shrinkwrap licenses evolved into "clickwrap." When you open up your new phone, you have to click through "I Agree" for whatever terms they have set. When you visit a website, you click through terms about privacy and cookies before you can access certain features. While there are legal limits on what a company can put into its clickwrap, the basic concept of including rules in this matter is enforceable in court. A term requiring you to give away your pet bird to use a website is not going to fly, but a term about not cheating in an online poker game or else you forfeit your winnings will hold up. Beyond the typical terms of service used online, sites that provide a marketplace will have additional agreements to protect themselves, since they are dealing with numerous financial transactions. When money starts changing hands, everything gets more serious.

But what is contained in those agreements? You could always read them, but who has the time for that? In 2018, artist Dima Yarovinsky created an installation art piece titled *I Agree*, which consisted of several colored scrolls hanging on a wall that were the physically printed terms of service for various popular websites and apps. The documents were so long that the paper ran down the wall and across the floor of the room, illustrating the absurdity of how much language is contained on the screens that we swiftly click past. Even if you had the time to read these epic novels of rules, you could be worried you won't understand all the legalese.

Lucky for you, some people have painstakingly reviewed these documents and written articles about their key terms. Since you are staking the future of business on access to the sites, the few minutes it takes to read up on the terms of service can have substantial pay off.

To sell on Amazon, for example, you must agree to the Amazon Business Solutions Agreement ("BSA"). If you have signed up as a professional seller on Amazon, you may have bound yourself already without realizing. The BSA was put in place in 2011 and governs ways a seller gets paid, requirements for insurance, a grant of a license to Amazon to use your trademarks on their site, a release of Amazon from liability, an agreement to indemnify Amazon if something goes wrong, and a confidentiality agreement. There are terms also governing your products, product listings, delivery, Amazon's customer guarantees, and charges and fees Amazon can issue.

These terms of service are not negotiable. The basic idea is that, if you don't like the rules, don't use the service. However, companies like Amazon are essential for many small and large businesses alike. Amazon won't change the terms, but you will be more successful if you know what is governing because you can plan for the charges, avoid violating terms you might otherwise not have known existed, and be prepared for when a claim is required to go through Amazon's own dispute resolution system. For Amazon, and all the other companies and apps you use, you should have a sense of what you have agreed to before something flares up and you get blindsided.

ONLINE DISPUTE RESOLUTION

You may have purchased something online in the past that turned out to be different from what you expected you were buying. Maybe the product was smaller than advertised, did not work as intended, or was broken. People have been burned before when buying what appears to be great deals on furniture online only to receive doll house accessories. If you bought from a third-party site, you are left attempting to resolve the dispute with the seller. Because the dollar value for many online sales is relatively low, or those sales are one-off purchases, there is a practical challenge in going after a seller. This is something the larger sites have tried to solve.

Many side hustlers and small businesses selling goods will use Etsy, eBay, or Amazon. These sites each have programs to handle disputes between buyers and sellers. Etsy has a case system where issues can be presented and handled. eBay uses their technology-assisted Resolution Center to hear disputes. Amazon uses their A to Z Guarantee Buyer Dispute Program. Each of those programs is aimed at resolving problems that exist above the level of an angry email from a buyer but below the level where one is seriously considering legal action in court. The point of each is to provide a platform to resolve problems, but unfortunately, simply utilizing them can impact your standing in the company's eyes.

You should become familiar with these dispute resolution systems and take them seriously. Although not courts in a traditional sense, they can operate similarly. Failure to participate or being involved in too many disputes can result in restrictions, suspensions, or even termination from the site. If you rely on a marketplace for your business, you must respect its rules and systems, since the punishments could have severe impacts on your business.

Lesson 7 Takeaways...

✓ Avoid making misleading or false statements about your business and that others, both online and off.

✓ If you use an online service or marketplace, take a few minutes to understand the rules governing your use and the process for resolving disputes.

✓ The terms of service are generally not negotiable, but you can navigate wisely by knowing the rules.

LESSON 8

WHEN YOU PAY YOURSELF, REMEMBER TAXES

When you start making money, it probably will not be consistent. You might go weeks without an order. You might receive a huge new client that pays upfront for six months of work. It's unpredictable. In either case, there are necessary expenses to keep operations going. Running your business is not free. You have to order supplies, pay rent for warehouse space, pay for your website, and more. You also will reinvest in the business to help it grow. You might buy a new sewing machine, take a course on marketing, or get a label-printing machine. Ultimately, your business will be developed enough to afford to pay yourself some of that hard-earned cash.

New entrepreneurs often ask: How do I actually pay myself? Receiving money from your business is a primary motivation for starting one, and although the actual process is simple, the answer to this question requires some planning. You will need to consider your specific tax situation to determine what is best, but there are some essential concepts that will apply to everyone.

PAYING YOURSELF

Employees of businesses are paid salaries. With your business, you can also pay yourself a salary. The benefit of paying yourself through salary is that you will withhold taxes owed through the business and that benefits are automatically paid out of the gross amount. If you pay a salary, you are less likely to face self-employment taxes, which are the way that the government still collects Social Security and Medicare taxes on people that own their own business. Even if it's your business, taking a salary as an employee means you have to comply with tax withholding.

The other main method to pay yourself is to take a draw. An owner's draw refers to simply taking money out of a business account and moving it into a personal account. An owner's draw can be either profits that the business has generated or money that the owner previously contributed to the business to help it operate. A draw from profits is subject to your payment of taxes. It will also potentially subject you to self-employment taxes.

Once you have generated enough money in your business to pay yourself, you might choose to take a salary, a draw, or even both. Before you pay yourself anything, you will want to ensure there are enough funds left in the business to pay its expenses, fund future orders, and cover any tax liabilities owed.

SIDE HUSTLE LAW

Defunding your business such that it cannot pay its bills will lead to serious trouble. As the owner, you will sometimes have to sacrifice your own income for benefit of the business.

SEPARATE BUSINESS ACCOUNTS

From the start, you need a separate bank account for the business. Opening a bank account for a small business is a simple and painless process, so do this right away. You will not only want to use this account to pay business expenses, but you will want to use it to receive the revenue your business generates. It is important that you keep your personal expenses separate from the business. It helps you easily track your revenue and expenses when it comes to creating financial, accounting, and tax-related reports. If you have any partners or investors, it is even more crucial that you avoid commingling your personal funds with business funds, as you will owe the other owners of the business fiduciary duties. The last thing you want is an IRS audit or a partner's lawsuit to have an excuse to dive deep into your personal financial information and create hours upon hours of work and expenses to unravel and defend.

If you are operating an LLC or a corporation, keeping your finances separate is also a significant factor in retaining the "limited liability" status. Commingling personal and business finances can lead to a breakdown of that special protection, which was the primary reason you spent money to incorporate in the first place. The same is true if you underfund the business such that it cannot pay its ongoing obligations like invoices, payroll, or loans. If you treat the business as a piggy bank, don't adequately fund it to pay its debts, and ignore the important separation between business and personal assets, you can lose your limited liability "veil" and become personally liable.

PERSONAL AND BUSINESS TAXES

The substantial majority of side hustles will follow a "pass through" taxation status. This will mean that the business income and taxes will be addressed on the owner's personal tax returns. If you are not taking only a salary, it also means you will have to think about taxes throughout the year. If you have only ever worked a typical job before, you could be surprised by having to think about taxes more than ever before.

As an employee, your employer is required to withhold income tax. Those withholdings will determine whether you owe any more taxes (or are owed anything back) at the end of the year. Although we typically only think about taxes in April, since that is the standard deadline to file tax returns, the reality is that you and your employer are paying taxes on your income all year by way of your employer's withholdings, which is what your year-end W-2 form shows. If you ever worked as a contractor, you would have received a 1099 form, which indicates that you have been paid for work but that no taxes have been withheld. Additionally, if you have a taxable account for investing, or even a savings account at a bank, you will have encountered paying taxes on your gains.

If you are running a business, no one else is handling taxes during the year. You are responsible for tracking, reporting, and paying taxes in the correct amounts. This requires making estimated calculations about what you will make, and as a result, what you might owe. If you are estimated to owe $1,000 or more in federal taxes, then you are required to make quarterly payments to the IRS. Failure to make these payments can lead to interest and penalties. There are easy ways to make the payments to the IRS, including making payments electronically.

The problem that comes up in all businesses, but especially new small businesses, is that you will not have a predictable amount of income to make estimated earning possible. Revenue and cash flow can be erratic. You might get a huge order unexpectedly cancelled, or you might get featured in the newspaper, with your sales exploding a few days later. In either event, you have to do your best to keep the tax authorities happy. Stay on top of this so you can temper the unexpected.

TRACK YOUR DEDUCTIONS

Not all is lost when it comes to taxes. There are crucial deductions that can be applied against your business income to reduce the taxes you will owe. Keep track of all your business expenses to drive down your taxable income number as low as possible.

There are a host of potential deductible expenses to claim. Some of the most common types include:

- Website hosting, domain name, and design expenses;
- Phone and internet that are used for the business;
- Business travel expenses and mileage;

- Supplies used in the business;
- Wages paid to employees;
- Insurance premiums; and
- Professional fees for lawyers and accountants.

On the personal side, you can put more income into tax-deferred investments, like a 401k, individual retirement account, or health savings account. Although it is historically a red flag for the IRS to audit, you could also consider whether the home office deduction applies for your business.

Like many Americans, you are probably doing your taxes yourself with tax preparation software, going to a tax preparation chain, or calling a relative to help you. Once you are making enough in a side business to justify the expense, you are hard pressed not to hire a professional. Taxes are serious, and things get much more complicated when forms and schedules start piling on to your tax return. It is money well spent to get piece of mind, and a good accountant can give you tips to save on your taxes that end up paying for themselves.

Lesson 8 Takeaways...

✓ Keep your business accounts separate from your personal ones. This is important for financial, legal, and tax reasons.

✓ If you made money, you'll owe taxes. Plan accordingly and determine whether you'll need to make estimated tax payments during the year.

✓ Track all your business spending. Many of these expenses will be deductible and lower your tax burden.

LESSON 9

IF YOU HIRE HELP, DON'T MISCLASSIFY EMPLOYEES

Hiring help is a huge step for any business. By hiring an employee, you are going full circle—what may have started as something you worked on while holding down your own job has become an opportunity to create a job for someone else. This is a huge milestone for your business, even if you are only bringing someone on part-time. You are now a boss. There are many management, leadership, and psychological concepts that come up when you take on this role. There are also legal ones.

In the United States, there is a vast array of federal employment laws that govern workers nationwide, but there are also specific state laws providing stricter requirements on a host of topics. Plus, employment law is not only a matter of the statutes passed by Congress or state legislatures, as there are also orders and regulations promulgated by executive agencies like the Department of Labor.

Employment law is a field ripe with potential problems. There are laws regarding payment methods, meal and rest breaks, overtime hours, minimum wage, safety, harassment, discrimination, hiring, termination, and more. Not to mention taxes, employee benefits, and insurance matters. On top of this, there are laws that incentivize workers to bring private claims for violations of their rights. This includes recovering attorney's fees for bringing a lawsuit, which means an employee's barrier to filing a claim is reduced. In light of all this, when you hire a worker, you need to appreciate the scope and potential impact of this decision.

Not all workers in a business are employees. One of the most important points to understand is the distinction between employee and independent contractor. Many business owners think the distinction only involves the decision to provide one tax form versus another. Rather than directing the classification, the tax form must follow the worker's proper classification. That is, a business owner cannot change a worker's status simply by giving them a different tax form. There are many factors at play.

WHAT IS THE DIFFERENCE?

You need a job done. That's the reason you are seeking help. You may pay an employee and an independent contractor for same or similar work. As alluded to above, one of the basic differences between an employee and an independent contractor involves tax treatment.

It is generally less expensive for a workplace to use a contractor over an employee because they are not required to make tax contributions or provide other employee benefits. This causes many businesses to think they will avoid those added expenses by paying a worker as a contractor whether or not it is proper. But a worker's tax treatment is not something the employer can choose; instead, it is the worker's role in the business and evaluation of a host of facts that inform which tax treatment is required.

This is where the tax forms come in. Workers are provided an information return at the end of any year where they earned money from some person or entity. The W-2 form is the tax document issued by an employer to its employee, which reflects what taxes have been withheld on the employee's behalf. Alternatively, if one has been working as an independent contractor, they may receive a 1099 form. The 1099 form states only the amount paid to the worker and acts as a record that those payments were made during the year. Yet, as a contractor, one will not have had any money withheld on their behalf to cover the taxes. Instead, the 1099 contractor is responsible for handling their own tax payments. The flip side for an independent contractor is that they can deduct expenses, since they are technically self-employed. Mileage, supplies, and other items can be claimed on their taxes to reduce the amount ultimately owed just as if they were a small business. A W-2 employee cannot claim those types of deductions, since they are instead taken by the employer.

At the same time, tax treatment is only one aspect of what distinguishes someone as an employee or an independent contractor. Employees also benefit from fairly expansive protections related to wage amounts, payment methods, working conditions, and hiring and firing. Independent contractors, on the other hand, are not necessarily afforded the same protections. As with taxes, some businesses try to call their workers independent contractors to avoid implicating other employment laws.

TEST FOR EMPLOYEE VERSUS INDEPENDENT CONTRACTOR

Unfortunately, there is no black-and-white formula to determine whether someone is an employee or an independent contractor. Like many parts of the law, the issue is grey and dependent on the facts. Further, the test for employee versus independent contractor depends, in part, on who is asking. The Internal Revenue Service uses a right-to-control test to assess tax liability related to the people working for a business. At the same time, the various states also have tests under state law to determine status for worker's compensation, unemployment insurance, and other employment laws.

Some states follow the "A-B-C test." As of 2018, this includes California pursuant to a decision by the California Supreme Court in *Dynamex Operations West, Inc. v. Superior Court of Los Angeles*. The A-B-C test says that a worker will be considered an employee unless the company can prove:

(A) that the worker is free from the control and direction of the hiring entity in connection with the performance of the work, both under the contract for the performance of the work and in fact;

(B) that the worker performs work that is outside the usual course of the hiring entity's business; and

(C) that the worker is customarily engaged in an independently established trade, occupation, or business of the same nature as the work performed.

The California decision created a fair amount of turmoil across many industries that regularly used independent contractors for the "usual course" of their business. This included major impacts on barbershops and salons, tattoo parlors, yoga studios, and many more. Under the A-B-C test, these types of businesses cannot use a "contractor" to perform the typical work of the business, so the business is forced to hire the worker as an employee and follow strict employment laws regarding wages, meal and rest periods, and insurance. While those laws are clearly important for protecting employees, many industries that do not fall neatly into a 9:00-to-5:00 style "clock-in/clock-out" approach have been greatly impacted. The decision has also caused turmoil for gig economy companies like Uber and Lyft, along with many legal battles over whether they are able to call their drivers "contractors," or whether they legally are employees. The industries that previously followed alternative schedule and pay structures have been scrambling to figure it out, given the misclassification concerns.

MISCLASSIFICATION

This distinction is vitally important because a business can face harsh penalties if it improperly classifies an employee as an independent contractor. There are federal and state agencies that can pursue claims against businesses that misclassify employees, as well as offering employees the ability to file a claim themselves in a simplified agency proceeding.

Misclassification includes potentially violating laws governing minimum wage, payment terms, overtime, meal and rest periods, unemployment insurance, worker's compensation, and fair employment laws. These often have penalties beyond the actual damage the employee incurred, which means the total amount owed for the violation can grow substantially. While a $20 per hour employee might only be owed an extra $10 per hour for the extra overtime they worked and were owed, the penalty for each of those hours could amount to thousands of dollars on top of other violations. If the IRS gets wind, there can be claims for back taxes, interest, and penalties. Beyond this, there are hosts of private attorneys that are hungry to take cases against businesses that misclassify employees. There are incentives in the law, such as rewarding the employee their attorneys' fees, which increase the chance of a case being brought.

Even if it seems unlikely, the damage that can happen due to not treating employees properly under the law can ruin your business. Having extra sets of hands is important and necessary to grow your business, but it is not something that should be taken lightly and you should take care to determine the status of any worker you hire.

CHARACTER EXAMPLE

Sara needs help fulfilling orders. With her designs finalized, she has been purchasing the plush toys in bulk orders from her manufacturer and storing them in her garage. She has set up some foldable tables and has plenty of shipping materials, but she doesn't have enough time in the day to get everything done.

Sara is interested in hiring someone to show up at her house a couple of days a week to take care of the orders she is receiving. She plans to give them a key to the side door of the garage. She says they need to arrive at exactly 7:30 AM and work for five hours. She says she wants them wearing non-slip shoes since the garage floor is smooth, and she has specific instructions for how to carry out the tasks. She has a laptop in the garage and created a user account for the worker. She wants them to log onto the email account that receives sales orders from the website, print out a shipping label from the computer printer, pull the plushie from the organized shelves lining her garage, and pack the item with tissue paper, a business card, and a sticker. She tells the worker to then fill up her car with the day's orders and drive to the post office. While there, the worker is also supposed to get any mail that came to company P.O. box.

Is Sara hiring an employee or an independent contractor? On these facts, she might be hiring an employee. She is requiring them to show up a certain time, she is exercising control over how they do their job, and the work itself might be considered a typical function of an e-commerce business. Nothing about the work relies on independent skills, like plumbing or accounting. Sara will need to be mindful of employment laws, taxes, and insurance that relate to having an employee work for her business. Otherwise, she needs to consider whether she could structure the job in a manner that does not invoke these factors.

Later, Sara finds someone to help produce animated video content featuring her characters. She gives the worker a deadline and a general idea of what she wants the animations to look like, the art style, and story. She tells them the poses she wants and what the characters are going to do. The worker works remotely from their house but checks in by phone and email every few days to inform Sara on progress of the work.

Is this an employee or a contractor? In this instance, the worker is more likely a contractor. Sara is not exercising control over how the worker does the job, just the outcome she wants. Her normal business is creating and selling plush toys and children's books online. She doesn't create the video pieces herself but directs with the ideas she wants. This isn't part of her usual course of business, but rather a service she needs fulfilled involving the worker's independent skills. She could still hire the animator as employee, but under these facts, she can likely structure the project for a contractor.

Hiring staff is one of the biggest events in the life of a small businesses because it signals that you have grown to a point where the work you have exceeds your capacity. With all the potentials for problems, you will need to read up on the various employment issues, including hiring, firing, workplace rules, wage and hour laws, and everything in between.

Lesson 9 Takeaways...

✓ Hiring workers is a big step for any business.

✓ Ensure that your employees are properly classified for tax, benefits, and other employment purposes. Consider the role, the job duties, and the level of control you exercise over the work.

✓ Giving someone a W-2 form or a 1099 form is not what determines whether someone is an employee or a contractor. You have to consider the nature of their work to determine how you treat them under the law.

CONCLUDING THOUGHTS

You have made your way through these nine lessons for starting and growing your side hustle or small business. Some of the information you may have heard before, and some of it may have been brand new. Let's recap and review some of the highlights.

Lesson 1: Don't violate your existing employment terms. A side hustle is, by definition, on the side. Before you blow it with your day job, check with your employer's policies or agreements that might impact your business and how you can operate it. Exclusivity, work-for-hire, and confidentiality are a few of the terms that may come into play.

Lesson 2: Obtain the necessary licenses and permits. Every type of business needs some interaction with the government, even if it is only a general business license. Depending on the service or product you offer, you may have multiple levels of government agencies looking at what you do. You can only fly under the radar for so long. Don't hurt your business or customers by risking an unexpected and preventable shut down.

Lesson 3: If you want a business partner, plan appropriately. Partners can complement your strengths and increase your chance of success while also providing you a shoulder to lean on when times get tough. However, we are all human, and difficulties can arise with expectations, assumptions, and communication. You will want a solid plan in place in the event you part ways with your partner to minimize the disruption on the business.

Lesson 4: Choose the right entity for running your business. There are many forms that a business can take. Some registered entity types will provide you with liability protection by putting up a wall to better separate your personal and business assets. But depending on the industry you are in, a corporation or LLC is not always necessary, especially when you are starting off. You can always convert your business form when the advantages of formal registration are more applicable.

Lesson 5: Consider buying insurance. There are multiple types of business insurance policies available, and they don't have to be outrageously expensive. While you hope to never need them, insurance can help you hedge against risks that you will face. A commercial landlord or company you start doing business with may even require that you obtain coverage.

Lesson 6: Understand the basics of intellectual property. The primary forms of intellectual property come into play for most businesses. These are copyrights, trademarks, patents, and trade secrets. You will either be seeking to protect your own intellectual property, or you will be trying to avoid violating someone else's. Make sure you properly license content that belongs to others.

Lesson 7: Watch what you say, even online. False and misleading statements are legally actionable. When you have a business, you become more of a target. There are rules governing the various online services and sites we use, so you should be familiar enough to navigate them and interact on the sites appropriately.

Lesson 8: When you pay yourself, remember taxes. Businesses can make payments to their owners in multiple ways. No matter what, you will owe taxes if you made any money in a given year. Keep your business and personal accounts separate and don't treat your business as a piggy bank.

Lesson 9: If you hire help, don't misclassify employees. The test between employee and contractor is not whether you give them one tax form or another. Instead, it depends on the nature of the work you have them performing and how it is performed. Employment is a huge step that signals that your business has reached a level where you are providing a job for someone else.

You start off the side hustle journey looking to add something to your life by pursuing a passion project or making some extra money. Like many entrepreneurs before you, your side business could end up replacing your day job and even creating jobs for others. This book has hopefully provided insight into the legal areas that your small business will encounter at some point during its existence. Knowing where the land mines are will help you steer around them.

Of course, the law is not the only place where issues happen in a business. You may struggle with personal issues, like handling the impact of negative reviews or feeling imposter syndrome when you see some success. You may also struggle with interpersonal issues, like if your partner stops talking with you or you become angry with a worker that makes repeat mistakes. You may struggle with more systemic issues in your business, such as problems with quality control, timely delivery, or crashing websites.

There are problems everywhere, and you will continue to face roadblocks and challenges. No one said this would be easy! But this should not stop you from pushing forward. Similar to the law, you can reduce the chance of encountering problems through education, awareness, and action. It is when you enter a false complacency and ignore the world around you that you can hit full stop.

We have followed Myra, Luis, Sara, and Alex to emphasize that every situation is different. There is no one-size-fits-all advice—legal or otherwise. Business involves people, and people are unique and unpredictable. That is both a curse and a blessing. Throughout your experience, remember that you are not alone. There are always resources and other people willing to help or share stories. Call someone that you admire and ask to take them to lunch. Schedule a meeting with someone that is performing at the level you want to be. Pick up a book about a new topic that will help your business expand. Look for support in online communities. Although it can be ruthless at times, most people will want to see you succeed.

You don't need these lessons just to mow some lawns in your neighborhood and grab quick cash. You can scrape by going through the motions. However, you won't be satisfied making pocket change if you have the itch to start and grow a business. You have bigger goals in mind. You have dreams of being your own boss, creating something you are proud of, and building financial stability. You are an entrepreneur.

ABOUT THE AUTHOR

MYLES TAYLOR is an attorney in northern California representing entrepreneurs and businesses of all sizes. He is a firm believer that even an ounce of preventative work and planning can help avoid massive legal problems in the future. He can be reached at: Contact@SideHustleLawBook.com.

WANT MORE TIPS?

If you are interested in learning more, be sure to check our website at <u>SideHustleLawBook.com</u> to sign up for our mailing list and follow our social media.

When new content becomes available, you'll be the first to know.